DATE DUE

NO 15 '00			

DEMCO 38-297

Handbook
of job facts

Fifth Edition

Compiled by Carole J. Lang
Guidance Department

S R A

SCIENCE RESEARCH ASSOCIATES, INC.
Chicago, Palo Alto, Toronto, Henley-on-Thames, Sydney
A Subsidiary of IBM

CONTENTS

INTRODUCTION

In a modern industrial society, a person's occupation is not only a way of making a living but also a way of life. Nearly half of a man's waking hours for forty years or more are taken up with his work. This statement is equally true for the single woman, and even married women are working an average of thirty years. The experiences a person has during these thousands of working hours affect every aspect of his life: his attitudes toward society, his friends and acquaintances, where he lives, what he does with his leisure time. In addition, his prestige in the eyes of others and his role in society are determined largely by his occupation. A young person's choice of a career is thus one of the most important decisions of his life.

One of the functions of the guidance counselor —many would consider it the main function—is to assist young people in making this difficult and crucial choice. Concise, accurate, and up-to-date information about a wide range of occupations gives the counselor the background knowledge he needs to assist his clients well, and gives the student or job seeker the essential facts with which to make an intelligent decision. Not even a vast store of facts and figures about occupations, of course, can give assurance either of adequacy on the part of the counselor or of a wise choice on the part of the young person. Counseling is much more than the imparting of knowledge, and a career choice involves much more than memorizing facts and figures. Occupational information is a tool designed to help in the involved process of vocational guidance and rational career planning. If used with skill and intelligence it can, like any tool, be invaluable.

Occupational information can take many forms. Career novels, books on occupations, and occupational monographs, articles, briefs, pamphlets, and films all meet specific needs of counselors and young people. But an occupational summary—such as this book—offers certain advantages not found in any of the other forms. For the counselor and librarian, it can serve as a handy reference source for pinpointing the basic features and trends of a variety of significant occupations. The teacher of a course or unit in occupations can use the book to get an overview of the scope and diversity of the occupational structure and as an aid to selecting occupations or job families to be studied. The student can use it as a general guide to work knowledge, as a primer of basic occupational facts, and as a tool in selecting occupations or occupational fields for more intensive exploration. Finally, an occupational summary like this book can serve the job seeker as a practical handbook of facts and figures on earnings, job requirements, trends, and other pertinent data.

This edition of the *Handbook of Job Facts* contains concise summaries of basic data on 300 major occupations. The information is arranged in chart form under headings that can be read at a glance. The following topics are covered: a brief description of typical duties and functions; the main industries and areas of the United States where jobs in the occupation are found; number of men and women employed in the occupation; the usual educational and training requirements; qualifications needed to enter the occupation, including abilities, aptitudes, interests, and character traits; ways to find employment and the normal line of advancement; nationwide data on earnings, including average earnings or range of variation for beginning to experienced workers; and employment trends, detailing the increase or decrease of workers in the occupation and the amount of competition for available openings.

Several factors were considered in selecting occupations for inclusion in this book. Our chief criteria of selection were the importance of the occupation (in respect to size, prestige, and value to society) and the trend of employment (other things being equal, first choice was given to occupations in which workers are rapidly increasing).

The figures on numbers of workers in each occupation are reliable, conservative estimates based, for the most part, on data from the Bureau of Labor Statistics, from professional, technical, and labor organizations, and from other authoritative sources. The figures we used represent the number of employed workers rather than the total number in the labor force (those employed plus those actively looking for work). In certain occupations, especially those subject to large seasonal variations in employment, the number of employed may differ considerably from the number of persons in the labor force.

Other facts and figures in this book represent typical nationwide conditions or averages. As you use the charts, remember that conditions in your community may be quite different from those depicted. The column on earnings, for instance, will not tell you exactly what salaries are being offered in your community. It will give you the nationwide range. If you live in San Francisco, average salaries will be near the top of the range. If you live in a small town in Mississippi, local salaries may be near the bottom.

Occupations are listed in the body of the book by the most significant word in the title. Often this is the second or third word. The various kinds of engineers, for example, are listed together, as are the different kinds of managers and many varieties of clerks. In some cases the first word of the title was considered most significant, as in the case of hospital attendants and personnel workers. When searching for a specific occupation, look first in the body of the book under what you consider the most significant word of the usual occupational title. If you fail to locate the desired occupation, consult the Index.

Each occupation that appears in the book is listed in the Index under every significant word in its title. "Local Bus Drivers," for example, appears under "Drivers" as well as under "Bus." When there are two or more common titles for the same occupation, listings refer the reader to the title used in the chart.

For each occupation the charts also list the number of the SRA WORK Brief and the number of the SRA Occupational Brief describing the job in greater detail. (These briefs are in either the SRA Widening Occupational Roles Kit or the SRA Occupational Exploration Kit.)

Among the many ways in which a young person can use this book, one of the best is to go through it page by page, reading the special-qualifications column and studying the occupations that seem to suit his interests, abilities, and character traits. He can narrow down the field still further if he knows how much education he is going to acquire. If he does not plan to finish college, for example, not only will he stand very little chance of ever entering a professional occupation, but he may find it hard to get ahead in certain sales, managerial, and technical occupations.

Once you have decided on a few occupations that you think you would like and would be suited for, you will be wise to find out more about them and other occupations related to them. Study publications such as the SRA Job Family Booklets, occupational briefs, and career books and articles. You will find a variety of helpful material in the Widening Occupational Roles Kit and the Occupational Exploration Kit, both of which are available in many school libraries and guidance departments. Your counselor or librarian may be able to suggest other sources or related occupations to investigate.

To the reader inexperienced in the study of occupations, a word of caution is in order. Of the thousands of occupations in the United States, this book contains just three hundred. Of the dozens of facts about each occupation, we have selected only the most important. The occupations we have chosen, however, represent the overwhelming majority of those usually considered by high school students, and account for a large proportion of all workers other than the semiskilled and unskilled. Like every broad collection of information that attempts to present a great amount of material in limited space, this book cannot tell the complete story. For certain purposes, however, a pocket dictionary is more valuable than an encyclopedia.

We hope that counselors, teachers, and librarians who have used the handbook, as well as the new crop of career-conscious students, will find this edition even more helpful than its predecessors.

OCCUPATION	ACCOUNTANTS	ACTORS AND ACTRESSES
DUTIES	Compile, analyze, audit business records; prepare financial records and reports. May specialize in cost accounting, tax work, budgeting, auditing, systems and procedures.	Play roles in dramatic productions. May sing and dance. May give readings of plays, poems, speeches; teach dramatics or acting.
WHERE EMPLOYED	Accounting firms, business and industry, government, teaching, independent practice. Throughout U.S., with some concentration in cities.	Legitimate theaters, motion pictures, radio networks, TV and recording studios. Most acting jobs in Hollywood and New York. Amateur, semiprofessional, and some professional jobs throughout U.S., especially in stock companies, community theaters.
NUMBER OF WORKERS	More than 500,000 accountants, including 120,000 certified public accountants. Less than 20% are women.	About 17,000 professionals; 65% men.
EDUCATION AND TRAINING	College degree in accounting preferred. Junior colleges, business schools offer 2-year courses.	College major in drama the best preparation. Private acting schools, community theaters also give training and experience.
SPECIAL QUALIFICATIONS	High numerical ability, accuracy in detail work. Business and financial interests. Most states require 1 or 2 years experience to take exam for C.P.A. certificate.	Outstanding talent, clear, well-trained voice, poise, ability to memorize, ambition to succeed, imagination, perseverance, expressive ability. Good looks and reasonable intelligence help. Actors' Equity Association (union) membership required.
WAYS TO ENTER FIELD	Campus interviews, college placement services; want ads, civil service exams, direct application to accounting or other companies.	Play roles in high school, college theater. Try out for little-theater groups, summer stock companies, bit parts in Broadway, TV, movie productions. Watch daily call sheets; check with union.
CHANCE OF ADVANCEMENT	Excellent for college graduates, C.P.A.'s. May become senior or chief accountant, corporation executive. C.P.A.'s can start own practice.	Limited. Only those with exceptional talent, ambition, and breaks can hope to become full-time professionals.
EARNINGS	Start: $9500–$11,500. Experienced: $9000–$16,000. Chief accountants: $12,000–$25,000. Top: $25,000 and up.	Broadway minimum: $164.45 a week; $217.50 on road. Movie minimum: $120 a day. TV: $181.50 for half-hour program. Top stars: $100,000 a year.
SUPPLY AND DEMAND	About 32,000 openings each year during 1970s. Increased demand for college graduates, especially in tax and machine accounting. Women encouraged.	Many aspiring actors; few jobs. Many actors have to work at other jobs to make a living.
REFERENCES	OEK Brief No. 61 WORK Brief No. 1	OEK Brief No. 62 WORK Brief No. 2

ACTUARIES

Project and evaluate statistical probability of death, sickness, accident, loss; determine insurance premiums and benefits to ensure a profit for the company. Determine dividends. Construct statistical tables.

Life, property, and casualty insurance companies; consulting firms; government agencies; insurance rating bureaus. A few are self-employed as consultants. Most work in cities.

About 5000. Less than 3% are women.

College degree in math or actuarial science preferred. Courses in insurance, economics, business administration helpful.

Ability, interest in math. Good judgment, executive ability. For full professional status, must pass a series of actuarial exams in math and all phases of insurance.

Start out in summer job as actuarial clerk. Campus interviews, college placement service, direct application to companies, civil service exam.

Excellent for men who have passed exams. Can move up to chief actuary, start own consulting firm, become company executive.

Start: $8000–$9500. Experienced: $15,000. Top: $25,000 and up.

Shortage of qualified actuaries; demand is increasing. Opportunities excellent, especially for women who qualify.

OEK Brief No. 251
WORK Brief No. 3

ADVERTISING ACCOUNT EXECUTIVES

Handle relations between agency and its clients. Study each client's market, sales, and advertising problems; develop plan to meet client's needs; seek approval of proposed program. May write copy, develop artwork, or supervise others in doing so. May handle one large account or a number of small ones.

In 5700 advertising agencies throughout U.S. Most are located in fairly large cities, with New York and Chicago having the largest numbers.

Advertising agency workers total approximately 75,000; 1/3 women.

College education with liberal arts foundation plus advertising and marketing courses. Training will come automatically on the job as beginner moves up through other jobs to account executive.

Exacting: a sense of the dramatic, understanding of what motivates people, some writing ability, vision to see total effect of ideas, ability to communicate with others, maturity, experience, friendly and outgoing personality.

Apply direct to advertising agencies. Watch ads in *Advertising Age, Printers' Ink*, and daily newspapers. College placement service can be helpful; campus interviews. Try local advertising club. Most beginners start as copywriters, a few as junior contact men.

Move up from other agency jobs or from an advertising department to an agency. Assignment to larger, more difficult accounts. Sometimes an executive becomes a partner in the agency or opens own agency.

$8000–$25,000 or more, depending on size of agency, experience of account executive, talent, number of accounts he handles.

Expect steady increase in advertising agency employment. Once they are in an agency there is usually ample opportunity for capable men and women to become account executives. Keen competition.

OEK Brief No. 371
WORK Brief No. 4

ADVERTISING COPYWRITERS

Write headlines, text, and slogans for newspaper and magazine ads, radio and TV commercials, car cards, posters. May write advertising letters, brochures, pamphlets. May help choose artwork for ads.

Advertising agencies, retail stores, manufacturing companies, and other organizations with large volume of advertising. Most jobs are in big cities, especially New York and Chicago.

Total professional advertising workers: about 140,000.

College degree in liberal arts or business with some advertising and marketing courses is preferred but not always demanded.

Flair for writing, imagination, salesmanship, understanding of people and motivation. Must be able to work under pressure to meet deadlines.

Apply direct to ad agencies, stores, businesses. Some employment agencies specialize in placing advertising personnel. Want ads, personal contacts may also be effective.

Good for creative, hardworking men and women. Can advance to copy chief, account executive, advertising manager.

Start: $6500–$10,000. Experienced: $11,000–$26,000. Pay higher in agencies, lower in retail stores.

Moderate employment increase through 1970s. Competition keen for available openings. Best opportunity for women in retail stores.

OEK Brief No. 361
WORK Brief No. 5

OCCUPATION	AIR TRAFFIC CONTROLLERS	AIRLINE PILOTS AND COPILOTS
DUTIES	Give instructions, advice, and information to pilots concerning takeoff, landing, weather and flight conditions. Use radio, radar, and other electronic equipment to keep planes on course and prevent accidents or delays.	Operate plane on ground and in flight, watch instruments, maintain course. Make all preparations for flight, prepare flight plan, supervise crew. Responsible for safety of passengers and cargo. Copilots relieve pilots, watch instruments, plot flying course, compute flying time, keep flight log.
WHERE EMPLOYED	By Federal Aviation Administration, at airport control towers and traffic control centers along air routes throughout U.S.	Scheduled airlines throughout U.S. Most home bases are near large cities. Also charter and other nonscheduled lines, flying schools, federal government.
NUMBER OF WORKERS	About 19,600.	More than 27,000 pilots and copilots for scheduled airlines; all are men. About 18,000, some women, in general aviation.
EDUCATION AND TRAINING	High school graduation preferred. Applicants must undergo about 2 years of formal and on-the-job training.	High school diploma; some lines require 2 years of college, prefer degree. Attend flying school to get flying time for pilot's license.
SPECIAL QUALIFICATIONS	Good voice, at least 21, 2½ years experience in air-ground communications or related field; must pass physical, written exam, training course for FAA certificate. Calm temperament.	Must pass strict physical, written, practical exams for FAA license. Leadership, stability, alertness, good judgment, responsibility. FCC radio-operator permit needed for scheduled airlines work.
WAYS TO ENTER FIELD	Can get experience in air traffic control in Air Force or Navy, then apply to FAA or Civil Service Commission for physical and written exams.	Pilot training in armed forces helpful. After getting 500–1000 hours flying time, apply to airline personnel offices for flight engineer or copilot openings.
CHANCE OF ADVANCEMENT	Can advance from trainee to controller, coordinator, chief controller. Advancement beyond controller may be slow.	After 5–10 years, copilots on scheduled lines can advance to pilot. May become chief pilot, start own flying service or school.
EARNINGS	Beginners: about $7000. Experienced: $9500–$17,800. Chief controllers: top $24,000.	Among the highest-paid workers in nation. Pilots' average: $30,000–$37,000. Top: $48,000. Copilots: $27,000–$30,000 or more.
SUPPLY AND DEMAND	Moderate growth through 1970s. Competition is stiff. About 800 openings a year expected.	Several thousand openings annually on scheduled lines. Competition very strong for the better jobs.
REFERENCES	OEK Brief No. 345￼ WORK Brief No. 9	OEK Brief No. 31￼ WORK Brief No. 13

AIRLINE DISPATCHERS

Coordinate details of flight schedules and operations, inform pilots of weather conditions, see that safety rules are observed.

By commercial airlines throughout U.S. Most large airports are near big cities.

About 1200 dispatchers and assistants; few women.

2 years college or equivalent experience.

Good voice, alertness, good judgment, calm in emergencies. Must get FAA certificate.

After 2 years experience the FAA exam for dispatcher certificate can be taken.

Start as radio operator. Can advance to air traffic controller, assistant dispatcher, dispatcher. Advancement may be slow.

Dispatchers start at about $860–$1140 a month; can earn $1185–$1670 a month after 10 years.

Employment expected to increase slightly for dispatchers, decrease slightly for radio operators. Stiff competition for openings.

OEK Brief No. 266
WORK Brief No. 12

AIRLINE STEWARDESSES

Responsible for passengers' comfort: seat passengers, give instructions, bring magazines, answer questions, serve food and beverages, help sick people and those with small children. Check tickets and passenger lists, prepare flight reports.

Commercial airlines. Most home bases located near large cities.

About 35,600. Some men employed as stewards on international flights; a very small number on domestic flights.

High school diploma. Some college, nurses training, or business experience preferred. May attend company or commercial training school.

Single when hired, 19–27, average height and weight, attractive, good personality; must have poise, tact, good manners, resourcefulness.

Apply direct to airline personnel offices. Want ads often list stewardess openings.

On probation for 6 months. Girls with seniority get choice of base, better flights. May become first stewardess, instructor, recruiting representative.

Start: About $523–$645 a month. Experienced: $590–$836 a month. Get living expenses while away from home base; some free air travel.

High turnover; about 5000 openings a year. Competition very strong, but chances good for well-qualified applicants.

OEK Brief No. 120
WORK Brief No. 14

AIRLINE TRAFFIC AGENTS AND CLERKS

Take reservations over phone or in person, sell tickets, check baggage, keep records. Supervise loading and unloading, keep cargo and passenger records. Coordinate service, check passengers aboard, make announcements.

Scheduled airlines in downtown offices and at airports. Most work in or near large cities.

About 45,000 men and women.

High school diploma required, some college preferred. Beginners get 2–4 weeks formal training.

Good voice, personality, attractive appearance. Patience, liking for people, tact, good memory. Age 21–30 preferred.

Apply in person to airline personnel offices. Watch want ads.

Good for men, fair for women. Can become office supervisor, traffic representative, city and district traffic and station manager.

Start: $495–$674 a month. Experienced: $605–$771. Station managers: $510–$854.

Employment increasing. Many openings every year; moderate competition.

OEK Brief No. 298
WORK Brief No. 15

OCCUPATION	ANESTHETISTS	ANIMAL KEEPERS
DUTIES	Prepare patient, equipment, anesthetic for operation; calm patient and watch his condition closely during operation; administer anesthetic; check on patient in recovery room.	Clean cages; feed and exercise animals; help take care of sick animals.
WHERE EMPLOYED	Hospitals throughout U.S. Most jobs in or near large cities. About 15% provide their services on a free-lance basis.	Zoo, animal hospitals, research laboratories.
NUMBER OF WORKERS	14,550 certified anesthetists, smaller number of noncertified; 8% men.	No definite figures; both men and women. There are 150 zoos in the U.S.
EDUCATION AND TRAINING	High school diploma, at least 3 years in nursing school, 18 months in accredited school of anesthesia.	High school helpful.
SPECIAL QUALIFICATIONS	Scientific and mechancial aptitude, knowledge of anesthetics, calmness, responsibility, liking for people, ability to make quick decisions, accuracy.	Strong liking for animals a necessity; good health; stamina.
WAYS TO ENTER FIELD	Professional association maintains placement service; ads appear in professional journal. Nurses-placement agencies. Most are offered jobs before leaving school.	Direct application to zoos, animal hospitals, research laboratories. May have to take civil service exam.
CHANCE OF ADVANCEMENT	Can improve salary by moving to larger hospital, specializing in one kind of operation. Can become instructor, supervisor.	Good. Can advance from assistant keeper, to keeper, to head keeper.
EARNINGS	Vary greatly. About same as head nurse or nurse supervisor.	Experienced: about $4.30 an hour.
SUPPLY AND DEMAND	Shortage of anesthetists.	Many new zoos opening; others expanding. Outlook good.
REFERENCES	OEK Brief No. 241 WORK Brief No. 17	WORK Brief No. 18

ANNOUNCERS, RADIO-TV

Introduce programs; read commercials, news reports; conduct interviews; describe sports contests, special events; introduce musical selections; identify station. In small stations, may have writing, sales, technical duties.

With radio and TV broadcasting stations and networks throughout U.S. Some work on a free-lance basis.

More than 17,000; 80% in radio.

High school diploma required. Networks want liberal arts college graduates.

Attractive voice and (for TV) appearance. Dramatic sense, likable personality, ability to think quickly, reading skill, knowledge of grammar and pronunciation.

College placement service helpful. Watch want ads. Apply direct to stations. May start as page boy, technician. Federal Communications Commission 3d class, broadcast-endorsed license needed.

Good for those with personality, drive. Can move to large station, network; from radio to TV; specialize as disc jockey, news analyst; free-lance.

Radio: $155–$300 a week. TV: to $25,000 a year. Top men make $50,000 or more. Earnings depend on size of station and community.

Demand increasing moderately; most openings in radio. Keen competition for openings, even in small stations.

OEK Brief No. 280
WORK Brief No. 269

ANTHROPOLOGISTS

Study aspects of primitive and civilized culture such as language, religion, art, law, social organization. Can specialize in physical anthropology, archaeology, ethnology, linguistics. May teach, do research, write books and articles, do consultant work.

Most work as college teachers. Others work for museums, government agencies, research associations, foundations, and in private industry. Fieldwork may be done anywhere in the world.

About 3100, of whom 20 percent are women.

Graduate degree, preferably Ph.D., essential for professional positions. Fieldwork necessary for Ph.D.

Special knowledge and interest in social sciences and humanities, patience, liking for people, persistence, intelligence, ability to see relationships.

Personal recommendation of graduate school professor. College placement bureau, civil service exam, direct application.

Promotion likely to be slow. Advancement usually in terms of higher salary, shorter teaching hours, chance to direct research project.

Start: $10,000–$12,000 for Ph.D's. Average: about $15,500. May supplement earnings with royalties from books, consultant fees.

Demand is increasing rapidly for anthropologists with doctorates, but this field is smallest of the social sciences. Little competition for openings.

OEK Brief No. 197
WORK Brief No. 19

ARCHAEOLOGISTS

Excavate and study places where earlier civilizations are buried, to reconstruct history and customs of the people who once lived there. Study the remains of homes, tools, clothing, ornaments, and other evidences of human life and activity. May teach, write articles or books, or do consultant work.

Federal government agencies, universities, and museums are principal employers. A few state agencies, research associations, and foundations employ archaeologists too.

About 1500, mostly men. Women are most often in museum work.

Many full-time jobs are open to those with master's degree. A Ph.D. is preferable and is required for most teaching jobs.

Special knowledge and interest in social sciences and humanities; patience, persistence, especially in record keeping; meticulousness; inclination to be very observant; ability to train and supervise fieldworkers.

Personal recommendation of graduate school professors. College placement bureau, civil service offices, ads in professional journals.

Instructors can advance to assistant, associate, and full professor; move to a larger or more affluent university or museum.

Beginners with M.A. degree: about $10,000. Average for all archaeologists: $15,500.

Trained men and women in this field are in great demand; most needed are specialists in American archaeology.

OEK Brief No. 212
WORK Brief No. 21

OCCUPATION	ARCHITECTS	ARCHITECTS, LANDSCAPE
DUTIES	Plan, design, and oversee construction and remodeling of buildings and other structures. Consult with clients and contractors, prepare specifications and sketches. May specialize in residences, factories, commercial or civic buildings.	Plan grounds and landscaping of subdivisions; parks; housing projects; shopping centers; zoos and museums; parkways; industrial sites; resort, beach, and waterfront properties; playgrounds; golf clubs; civic centers, institutions, monuments. May teach.
WHERE EMPLOYED	Architectural companies, engineering and construction firms, government agencies, colleges and universities. Almost half are self-employed. Architects work throughout U.S., especially in urban areas.	Self-employed or work for architectural, engineering, city-planning firms; federal, state, or local government agencies; nurseries; colleges or universities. Work throughout U.S., especially in heavily populated areas.
NUMBER OF WORKERS	33,000 licensed architects; 4% women.	About 9900; 10%–15% women.
EDUCATION AND TRAINING	Usually 5-year program in college of architecture, plus 3 years apprenticeship before taking state licensing exam.	College degree in landscape architecture.
SPECIAL QUALIFICATIONS	Artistic and mathematical interest, ability. Creativity, mechanical aptitude, business sense, understanding of people; ability to determine spatial relations. Must get state license.	License required in a few states. Creativity, appreciation of beauty, business and administrative ability, interest in both art and nature.
WAYS TO ENTER FIELD	Through college placement offices, employment agencies, direct application to construction or architectural firms. During college, may work summers in architect's office.	College placement offices and architectural publications list openings. Civil service exams for government positions. Usually begin as junior draftsman.
CHANCE OF ADVANCEMENT	Start as junior draftsman or trainee, move up to chief draftsman, designer, construction supervisor, associate architect. Can start own practice.	Slow at first, to senior draftsman. Can become partner, start own business.
EARNINGS	Start: $6200–$8300. Experienced draftsmen: $7000–$13,000. Top: $25,000 or more.	Start: $7000–$9000. Experienced: $15,000–$20,000. Top: $25,000 or more.
SUPPLY AND DEMAND	Demand expected to increase considerably in next decade. Employment linked to construction.	More architects needed than graduate each year. Women encouraged.
REFERENCES	OEK Brief No. 64 WORK Brief No. 22	OEK Brief No. 187 WORK Brief No. 177

ASBESTOS AND INSULATION WORKERS

Cover ducts, pipes, tanks, furnaces, and the like .with insulation made of cork, felt, asbestos, fiberglass, or other material. Use hand tools to cut and to install insulation by pasting, taping, spraying, or stud welding. May repair insulation in factories.

Most work for industrial and commercial contractors in construction. Some do maintenance work in industrial plants. Throughout U.S., especially in industrial centers.

About 22,000; 3% women.

No specific formal education required. About 4 years of on-the-job training to become skilled journeyman.

Good health, physical stamina and average strength, mechanical ability, and skill with tools. Must pass practical exam for journeyman status.

Apply to union offices for information about trainee openings. May apply direct to insulation contractors, industrial plants in chemical, oil, rubber, or like industries.

Pay increases progressively during training. Skilled workers can become foremen, shop superintendents, estimators; open own contracting business.

Wage range: $5–$8 an hour. Average: $6.30. Trainees start at 50% of journeyman wage.

Growing occupation; demand depends on rate of building construction.

OEK Brief No. 307
WORK Brief No. 25

ASSEMBLERS IN ELECTRONICS INDUSTRY

Assemble electronic components and end products, by hand and using small hand tools, soldering, welding, automatic positioning. Use diagrams, models, color-coded parts and wires; may view color-slide guides and listen to recorded directions. May perform single operation or completely assemble a component; may assemble under magnifying glass or microscope.

Manufacturers of television sets, radios, hi-fi and stereo equipment, computers, tape recorders, hearing aids, communications and navigational apparatus, variety of military and space equipment, electronic components such as relays, switches.

Estimated at over 200,000, mostly women.

High school education and on-the-job training. For advancement, some technical school study will be helpful, and some plants offer in-service training programs.

Ability to work rapidly, steadily, with maximum accuracy; good vision, finger dexterity, patience, no objection to repetitive, sedentary work.

Apply direct to plants making electronic devices or components. See state employment agency, newspaper want ads.

May become inspector, group leader, unit supervisor, troubleshooter, tester, experimental assembler, foreman, or technician.

Average, depending on type of production: $2.15–$3.75 an hour.

Expect rapid growth in employment through mid-1970s, plenty of jobs for those who are qualified.

OEK Brief No. 314
WORK Brief No. 26

ASTRONOMERS

Observe and study celestial bodies; may use telescopes, cameras, spectrometers, computers, other optical and electronic devices to collect, analyze and record astronomical data. May teach, do research, write articles and books.

Colleges and universities, planetariums and observatories, museums, government agencies, industrial laboratories throughout U.S.

About 1350; very few women. Only about 500 are full-time astronomers.

Undergraduate study in astronomy, physics, or math; graduate degree in astronomy required for professional positions.

Precise and logical thinking; aptitude for science, math, research, mechanics; good imagination; high degree of intelligence.

Personal recommendation of graduate school professors, civil service exam. Professional journals also have information about openings.

May start as research assistant, observer, computer while getting Ph.D. Advancement may be slow in colleges, observatories.

Start: with master's degree, $10,000–$11,500; with Ph.D., $13,000–$14,000. Average: $13,000. Some earn extra income through books, articles, consultant fees.

Excellent employment opportunities, especially in space programs of government and industry. Government research most favorable for women. Top jobs require doctorate.

OEK Brief No. 213
WORK Brief No. 27

OCCUPATION	ATHLETIC COACHES	BAKERY WORKERS
DUTIES	Coach team or individual sports. May specialize in one sport or one aspect of a sport. Plan, organize practice sessions and strategy. May teach physical education, health, academic subjects; make business arrangements; give press interviews.	Make bread, cakes, pastries, and other baked goods. In small bakeries, may perform all operations; in large ones, operate machines that mix, divide, mold, bake, and slice the dough or baked products. May specialize in one product.
WHERE EMPLOYED	High schools, colleges, professional teams, athletic clubs and associations. In rural as well as urban areas.	Large wholesale bakeries, specialty bakeries, retail bake shops, bakeries owned by food chains, hotels and restaurants, hospitals and other institutions.
NUMBER OF WORKERS	About 100,000 sports instructors and officials; nearly 33% women.	About 290,000 bakers and bakery production workers; 20% women.
EDUCATION AND TRAINING	College degree with credits in education and physical education. Graduate degree helpful for college coaches.	High school diploma, vocational school helpful. Most learn by on-the-job training; a few through a 3- or 4-year apprenticeship.
SPECIAL QUALIFICATIONS	Leadership ability, good judgment, fairness, even temper, physical stamina, good character, love of sports, expert knowledge of rules and strategies. Must have teacher's certificate.	At least 18, physical stamina. Most states require health or food handler's certificate.
WAYS TO ENTER FIELD	College placement bureau, personal recommendation. Start as assistant coach of college team, teacher-coach, or physical education instructor in high school.	Apply to union office, state employment service, direct to employers. Want ads may also be helpful. Learn trade in armed forces. New men usually start as helpers.
CHANCE OF ADVANCEMENT	Can move up from assistant to head coach; get college coaching job, become athletic director, school administrator, camp director.	Good chance to become specialist, skilled worker. Some become foreman, all-round baker, or start own retail bakery.
EARNINGS	Average: $10,500 for high school coaches; $20,000 for college coaches. Coaches of professional sports may earn $50,000 or more.	Vary widely according to area and employer. Average: $3.33 an hour. Foremen: $2.66–$4.93.
SUPPLY AND DEMAND	Demand increasing for qualified men and women; competition brisk for men's coaching jobs in top colleges and high schools.	Slow decline in total number of jobs because of increased mechanization. Best chances will go to skilled workers.
REFERENCES	OEK Brief No. 242 WORK Brief No. 28	OEK Brief No. 21 WORK Brief No. 36

BANK CLERKS

Deliver mail and records; keep files; handle checks, deposits, and withdrawals; maintain accounts and other records; type letters and reports; operate calculating, bookkeeping, and other business machines.

Commercial banks, mutual savings banks, the 12 Federal Reserve banks, and similar financial institutions. In towns and cities of all sizes.

More than 500,000 bank clerks, including 150,000 tellers. About 90% of bank clerks are women.

High school diploma required. On-the-job training may last a week to 5 months. Night courses helpful for advancement.

Accuracy, honesty, dependability. Politeness and attractive personality required for employees dealing with public. Clerical aptitude necessary to acquire speed, skill.

Want ads, employment agencies, direct application to banks. May start as a messenger, file clerk, transit or bookkeeping clerk, trainee machine operator.

Can advance to teller, supervisory positions. Chances good for those who can take responsibility.

Range: $70–$130 a week. Men generally are paid more than women.

Bank clerical jobs have high rate of turnover. About 30,000 openings a year expected. Prospects best for those who can operate electronic data-processing equipment.

OEK Brief No. 11
WORK Brief Nos. 37, 39

BANK OFFICERS

Administer banking services such as loans, trust funds, safety deposit services, investment counseling, checking and savings accounts. Officers include president, vice-presidents, cashiers, treasurer, junior officers.

Commercial banks, mutual savings banks, other financial institutions.

About 175,000 bank officers; 10% are women.

College degree in business or liberal arts required. Many banks have formal executive training programs.

Dependability, honesty, integrity, tact, prudence, good judgment, respectability. Logical mind and mathematical ability desirable.

Apply to personnel office of a bank. Most start as trainees in clerical positions such as teller, and are rotated among the departments as they gain experience.

It may take many years to become an officer. Advancement to top positions often depends on death or retirement of incumbent.

Executive trainees: $580–$750 a month. Junior officers: $8000–$15,000. Senior officers: to $50,000 or more. City banks usually pay more than those in small towns.

Banking is still a growing industry, and officers' jobs are increasing. Estimate 11,000 available each year. Competition is keen for both entry and top positions.

OEK Brief No. 46
WORK Brief No. 38

BARBERS

Cut customers' hair. May give shaves, shampoos, scalp massages, facials, occasionally sunlamp treatments. Shop may sell hair tonic and shampoo, offer shoeshine service. Owners manage shop, keep records, order supplies.

Independent barbershops and those in hotels, air and railroad terminals, department stores, office buildings. In towns and cities of all sizes.

About 180,000, including self-employed; very few women.

Must be barber school graduate, serve apprenticeship lasting 1 or 2 years. High school graduation helpful but not required.

Tact, patience, good humor, courtesy. Must pass exam for state license. Friendliness and a good personality can increase earnings through tips.

Barber schools have placement services. Apply to union if area is unionized. Want ads and state employment service also good sources of job leads.

Good chance to open own shop for ambitious man with some business ability.

Most are paid commission of 65%–75% for each haircut they give; tips extra. Average: $7800–$9000 a year. Top: $13,000 or more.

Moderate increase in employment expected. Average competition for openings, which number about 8000 a year.

OEK Brief No. 162
WORK Brief No. 40

OCCUPATION	BEAUTY OPERATORS	BINDERY WORKERS
DUTIES	Cut, style, shampoo, bleach, color, straighten, and wave hair. May give manicures, facials, and scalp massages; apply cosmetics. May specialize in one or more of these duties. Owners order supplies, keep records, supervise employees, make appointments.	Operate various bindery machines; perform hand operations in the binding process, such as collating, sorting, tipping-in. May be all-round bookbinder or specialize in one operation.
WHERE EMPLOYED	Beauty shops, department-store and hotel salons. Manicurists may work in barbershops. In cities and towns throughout U.S.	Binderies and binding departments of printing plants and publishing houses. Most work in cities, especially publishing centers such as New York, Chicago, Philadelphia, Boston.
NUMBER OF WORKERS	About 485,000; more than 10% men.	About 30,000 skilled bookbinders, 54,000 semiskilled workers. Well over half of bindery workers are women.
EDUCATION AND TRAINING	High school graduation helpful but not required. Must complete 6–12-month course in beauty school. A few states will accept 1- or 2-year apprenticeship.	High school plus formal apprenticeship of 4 or 5 years for skilled workers; on-the-job training of 2 years or less for semiskilled.
SPECIAL QUALIFICATIONS	16–18 minimum age, good health, physical stamina. Patience, tact, and a good personality helpful. Must pass exam for state license.	Physical stamina, hand-eye coordination, mechanical aptitude, liking for routine work.
WAYS TO ENTER FIELD	Many beauty schools have placement services. Other ways to enter: state employment service, want ads, direct application to beauty shops.	Apply to union office or direct to a bindery or printing plant.
CHANCE OF ADVANCEMENT	Can become a specialist in one aspect of beauty culture; shop manager; teacher; open own shop. Earnings increase with experience.	Fair. Can become inspector, supervisor, foreman.
EARNINGS	Most are paid weekly wage plus commission and tips. Beginning average: $5200 a year. Top: $15,000 or more for owners, managers, stylists.	Skilled: $2.69–$6.06 an hour. Semiskilled: $2.15–$3.41 an hour. Apprentices start at about half journeyman rate.
SUPPLY AND DEMAND	Occupation increasing. Specialists and skilled operators much in demand to fill 40,000 jobs a year. Competition average for beginning positions.	Skilled workers expected to decline slightly in number. Semiskilled openings will increase somewhat. Competition light.
REFERENCES	OEK Brief No. 112 WORK Brief No. 41	OEK Brief No. 56 WORK Brief No. 45

BIOCHEMISTS

Study the chemical substances and processes of living organisms. May specialize in one kind of substance or process. Do basic and applied research. May teach chemistry or biology as well as biochemistry.

Colleges and universities, medical schools and hospitals, research laboratories, government agencies, foundations, private industry.

Estimated 11,500 biochemists; 15% women.

Master's in biochemistry required for beginning professional positions; Ph.D. for research and teaching.

Scientific interest and aptitude, curiosity, reasoning and problem-solving ability, imagination, persistence, patience. Must pass civil service exam for government jobs.

Recommendation by college professors. College placement bureau, civil service office, want ads in scientific journals and newspapers, direct application to employer.

Excellent for talented researchers, teachers, men with administrative ability. More than in most fields, depends on ability.

Start: $6000–$8000 or more. Experienced: $10.000–$15,800.

Biochemists are much in demand and have practically no competition for jobs. Chances best for those with Ph.D.

OEK Brief No. 131
WORK Brief No. 42

BOILERMAKERS

Assemble, erect, dismantle, and repair boilers and other pressure vessels. Use power tools and devices such as oxyacetylene torches, welding equipment, power shears, and rigging equipment.

Boiler manufacturing companies, repair shops, and such industries as steel, railroads, construction, chemicals, electric power, and oil refining. Throughout U.S., but concentrated in industrial areas.

About 25,000.

High school diploma preferred. 4-year apprenticeship or on-the-job training to acquire skilled status.

Physical strength, stamina, mechanical ability, manual dexterity, tolerance for noise, odors, heights.

Apply to employer or union office. Can also locate openings through want ads, state and private employment agencies. Take civil service exam.

Fair chances for advancement to foreman, gang leader, or superintendent.

Journeyman wages: $3.28–$5.60 an hour.

Demand increasing moderately in maintenance and construction work. About 700 openings a year.

OEK Brief No. 316
WORK Brief No. 43

BOOKKEEPING WORKERS

Keep business records: make accounts payable, accounts receivable, profit and loss entries. Prepare reports and balance sheets. May prepare payroll and statements, handle bank deposits and withdrawals. May operate bookkeeping machines.

In almost every sizable business, government, and professional organization. General bookkeepers usually work in small organizations; machine operators in large ones such as banks, insurance companies, department stores.

More than 1.34 million; 90% women.

High school diploma usually required. Business school training or junior college preferred. On-the-job training often given.

Accuracy, liking for detail work, honesty, ability to work under pressure, good powers of concentration. Manual dexterity, good eye-hand coordination required for machine operation.

Placement office of business school, want ads, state and commercial employment agencies, direct application to employers.

Chances fair to advance to a supervisory position, such as that of head bookkeeper or office manager.

Starting average: $439 a month. Experienced average: $568. Men usually earn more than women for the same work.

Number of bookkeeping workers increasing rapidly. Expected need is 74,000 a year. Most new openings will be for machine operators.

OEK Brief No. 16
WORK Brief No. 46

OCCUPATION	BRICKLAYERS	BUILDING CONTRACTORS
DUTIES	Construct and repair structures such as walls, fireplaces, and partitions using brick, tile, terra cotta, and other materials. Erect scaffolds, check alignment of work. Use hand tools such as trowel, brick hammer, jointer.	Make estimates, prepare bids, sign contracts with customers to complete construction jobs, buy materials, hire and supervise workmen. Follow specification and architect's blueprints. Special-trade contractors specialize in one building trade or several related trades.
WHERE EMPLOYED	Most work for masonry and general contractors in the construction industry; a few in the glass, steel, and ceramics industries. Throughout U.S., but especially in cities and towns.	Self-employed: may head a company that specializes in home building, industrial building, commercial or office building. Special-trade contractors subcontract to do plumbing work, carpentry, and the like.
NUMBER OF WORKERS	About 200,000.	About 480,000 general and special-trade contracting companies.
EDUCATION AND TRAINING	High school diploma plus 3-year apprenticeship. Some learn through trade school courses, on-the-job training.	High school the minimum. College courses in building construction and business helpful. Many start as craftsmen in a building trade.
SPECIAL QUALIFICATIONS	Physical strength, stamina, manual dexterity, dependability, accuracy, no fear of high places. May have to pass exam for journeyman status.	Thorough knowledge of construction, business ability, responsibility, leadership and organizational ability, salesmanship.
WAYS TO ENTER FIELD	Apply to union, state employment agency, or direct to employer. Recommendation of friend or relative who is a bricklayer may be helpful in obtaining apprenticeship.	High school graduates start as apprentices in a building trade; college or technical school graduates, in a sales, office, or supervisory job with a large contractor.
CHANCE OF ADVANCEMENT	Good chance to become foreman, estimator, superintendent, or masonry contractor.	Contractors advance by expanding operations — getting more or larger contracts. Good chances for those with business sense.
EARNINGS	Union journeymen average $6.69 an hour. Apprentices start at 50% of the journeyman wage.	May be low to start. Experienced men earn at least $20,000–$30,000. Owners of large firms may make much more.
SUPPLY AND DEMAND	Occupation increasing moderately in number. About 8500 openings annually. Chances good for skilled men, but competition for apprenticeships is keen.	Demand depends on general economic conditions. Competition for small construction jobs is keen.
REFERENCES	OEK Brief No. 22 WORK Brief No. 48	OEK Brief No. 231 WORK Brief No. 50

BUILDING SERVICE WORKERS

Clean floors, furniture, equipment; wash windows; move furniture, refuse cans; make minor repairs. May operate electrical cleaning equipment. May do outside work such as mowing, shoveling, sweeping.

Throughout U.S. in schools, factories, apartment and office buildings, retail stores.

More than 1 million; 75% men.

No educational requirements. High school or vocational school training helpful.

Physical stamina; mechanical aptitude; responsibility; ability to work without supervision.

Apply to rental or realty office, building office, board of education. State employment services and union offices have listings of available jobs. May start as helper.

Limited. In buildings with large staffs may advance to supervisory position.

Average range: $1.65–$2.40 an hour. May work in more than one building for extra pay. Workers in apartment buildings may live rent-free.

About 70,000 job openings a year expected.

OEK Brief No. 101
WORK Brief No. 51

BUS DRIVERS, LOCAL

Operate commercial, charter, or government buses. Collect fares and transfers, make change, issue tokens or transfers. Answer questions about routes. May check operating condition of bus. Fill out records and reports.

Local transit companies, either private or city-owned. Many also work for school systems, charter bus companies, sightseeing companies, and government agencies. In cities and towns throughout U.S.

About 65,000; about ¾ work for commercial transit companies; few women. More than 200,000 part-time school bus drivers.

High school preferred. Bus companies give formal and on-the-job training lasting several weeks.

At least 21, good eyesight, coordination. Must have state chauffeur's license; pass written, physical exams. Friendliness and even temper helpful.

Apply direct to bus company or other employer. Want ads sometimes helpful. Usually start on the extra board with irregular routes and hours.

Mostly in terms of getting better route and more favorable hours. Some chance of promotion to instructor, dispatcher, road supervisor.

National average: $3.20–$4 an hour.

Demand slightly down for commercial bus drivers, up for school bus drivers. Average competition for openings.

OEK Brief No. 230
WORK Brief No. 189

BUS DRIVERS, LONG-DISTANCE

Operate long-distance or intercity buses. Check tires, water, and fuel before starting run; collect tickets or cash fares; announce stops; prepare records and reports. May load and unload baggage, make minor emergency repairs.

Commercial long-distance bus lines and charter bus companies. Most work out of large cities.

About 25,000.

High school diploma preferred. 2–6 weeks in company training school, plus on-the-job training with experienced driver.

Age 21–40, good eyesight, coordination, courtesy, emotional stability, alertness. One year driving experience, chauffeur's license; pass written, physical, driving exams.

Apply direct to bus company. New drivers usually start out on the extra board—making extra runs and substituting for absent drivers.

Poor. May take several years to get regular run. A very few become dispatchers, supervisors, or terminal managers.

Paid on mileage or hourly basis with guaranteed minimum. Average: about $9600.

Demand may increase moderately. Low turn-over reduces number of openings. Competition stiff for the better jobs.

OEK Brief No. 57
WORK Brief No. 190

OCCUPATION	BUSBOYS	BUYERS
DUTIES	Carry dishes, serving utensils, and trays of food. Keep side table stocked with silverware, condiments, napkins. Set tables, clear away dishes when customers finish eating. Clean cooking equipment, mop floors, arrange furniture. Help serve food and drinks.	Purchase goods to be resold at a price to cover expenses and provide a specified minimum profit. Select merchandise, develop sales techniques, keep records, maintain well-balanced stock of goods. May travel to market shows and exhibits.
WHERE EMPLOYED	Restaurants, dining rooms, cafeterias.	Department stores, specialty shops, mail-order houses, large retail chains. May be resident buyer, who remains permanently in the buying center, probably New York, studying the market and assisting visiting buyers.
NUMBER OF WORKERS	About 90,000, mostly men.	Indeterminate number. More than half of all department store buyers are women.
EDUCATION AND TRAINING	No special education requirements. Most restaurants give a week or more of on-the-job training.	High school education adequate, but college gives beginner an advantage. Work-study programs provide experience. College liberal arts, marketing, merchandising, retailing are helpful.
SPECIAL QUALIFICATIONS	In many places, must have health certificate. Physical stamina, neat appearance, willingness to work, alertness, courtesy.	Maturity, poise, good judgment, originality, creativity, curiosity, enthusiasm.
WAYS TO ENTER FIELD	Apply to restaurant or other eating place. Watch newspaper want ads. In some exclusive restaurants, busboys are chosen by the waiters.	Some start in salesclerk jobs. Some, college graduates particularly, start as buyer trainees. Direct application to stores is best entry route. Newspaper want ads and state employment service can be helpful.
CHANCE OF ADVANCEMENT	Good chance for busboy to become waiter. Bus girl can become cashier, possibly hostess.	After several years as assistant buyer, can be promoted to buyer. May become resident buyer or merchandise manager, or get an executive position. Some move to larger or more prestigious department or store.
EARNINGS	Busboys, 55¢–$1.75 an hour; girls, slightly less. In some eating places waiters share tips with busboys.	Executive trainees: $6300–$7500. Experienced: $9000–$14,000. Top: $35,000 or more.
SUPPLY AND DEMAND	Many job openings for busboys because of high turnover. Some competition for openings when jobs are scarce.	Demand for buyers will continue upward with further expansion in retailing. Promotion from within provides ample supply most of the time.
REFERENCES	OEK Brief No. 317 WORK Brief No. 52	OEK Brief No. 284 WORK Brief No. 310

CARPENTERS

Erect wooden framework of buildings; install doors, stairs, floors, and wooden trim. Construct forms, sheds, and other wooden structures. Repair items made of wood or similar material. May specialize in one aspect of carpentry.

Most work for carpenters in the construction industry. Others do construction work in factories, government installations, mines, shipyards, and large buildings. Many are self-employed.

About 830,000, almost all men.

High school diploma desirable. 4-year apprenticeship or longer period of on-the-job training.

Manual dexterity, mechanical aptitude, agility, good health and stamina, coordination, patience, liking for outdoor work.

Apply direct to union office, contractor, construction company, other employer. Want ads and state employment offices sometimes helpful.

Good for skilled men. Can become foreman, supervisor, contractor; do free-lance jobs for homeowners.

Average union minimum wage: $6.42 an hour. Apprentices start at 50%–60% of journeyman wage.

46,000 replacements needed annually. Expect slight increase in number of jobs. Apprenticeships hard to get in some areas.

OEK Brief No. 23
WORK Brief No. 54

CASHIERS

Take money, make change; keep records of receipts, expenditures, checks; prepare bank deposits. May pay small bills, keep and balance books, cash checks, and the like. Use cash register and, often, change-making machine.

Restaurants, cafeterias, grocery stores, drugstores, theaters, hotels, department and variety stores, insurance companies, loan companies, public utilities, and a variety of other businesses.

About 850,000, of whom about 1/3 are part-time workers; 10% men.

High school diploma preferred but not always required.

Knowledge of basic arithmetic, ability to make change rapidly, accuracy, honesty, dependability, finger dexterity, neat appearance, pleasant personality.

Watch newspaper ads. Apply to restaurants, theaters, stores, and other employers.

Limited. Can become salesclerk, department supervisor, hostess, bookkeeper; but may need additional training.

$1.60–$3 or more an hour. May get free meals, discounts, other benefits.

Employment increasing. Expect to need 75,000 a year. Considerable competition because little or no special training needed.

OEK Brief No. 12
WORK Brief No. 55

CATERERS

Plan parties for clients—help select food, decorations, entertainment; may prepare food, make deliveries, set up for parties, attend parties or group functions to see that all runs smoothly. May operate vending truck and sell food.

Catering establishments, hotels, schools, restaurants, clubs. May own business.

Several thousand.

High school necessary; college useful for supervisory positions. Junior colleges, 4-year colleges, vocational schools offer programs in food service.

Knowledge of food and the food industry; even temperament; physical stamina; organizing ability; good business sense.

Want ads, direct application, college placement services.

Good. May advance to managerial position or open own business.

Range: $4500–$40,000, depending on ability and education.

Demand for catering services will continue high through the 1970s.

OEK Brief No. 383
WORK Brief No. 56

OCCUPATION	CEMENT MASONS	CHEMISTS
DUTIES	Finish exposed surfaces of concrete constructions such as sidewalks, floors, highways. Direct pouring of cement; level, tamp, and smooth the surface; finish edges. Use hand and power tools. May repair or patch old concrete.	Study composition and chemical properties of substances, and processes of chemical change. May do basic and applied research, analysis, testing, teaching, selling, administration. May specialize in one branch of chemistry.
WHERE EMPLOYED	General contractors, cement contractors, government and city public works agencies, public utilities, and large manufacturing companies.	Most work in manufacturing or processing industries such as the chemical, drug, plastics, soap, and metals industries; others in universities, government agencies, research institutes. Some are consultants.
NUMBER OF WORKERS	About 65,000.	About 137,000, 5% women. By far the largest scientific profession.
EDUCATION AND TRAINING	High school diploma desirable. 3-year apprenticeship is the best way to learn trade, but may learn through on-the-job training.	Bachelor's degree essential. Ph.D. needed for top jobs in research, teaching, and administration.
SPECIAL QUALIFICATIONS	Physical strength, stamina, liking for outdoor work, manual dexterity.	Scientific interests and aptitude, accuracy, curiosity, patience, thoroughness. Creativity, writing, and administrative ability will speed advancement.
WAYS TO ENTER FIELD	Apply to cement or general contractor, union office, or company that hires cement masons. May start as laborer or helper.	Campus interviews while still in college, college placement bureau, employment agencies, ads in newspapers, notices in chemical journals, direct application.
CHANCE OF ADVANCEMENT	Fair chance to become foreman, superintendent, cement contractor. Some do free-lance work for homeowners.	Good opportunities in research, administration, production for those with advanced degrees.
EARNINGS	Average union minimum wage: $6.02 an hour. Apprentices start at 50%–60% of journeyman rate.	Starting average in industry, depending on education: $8500–$13,500. Top: $20,000 or more. Highest salaries in industry, lowest in education.
SUPPLY AND DEMAND	Demand increasing as more concrete is used in building construction. Expect over 3500 openings annually.	Demand considerably greater than number of graduates. Best opportunities for chemists with advanced degrees.
REFERENCES	OEK Brief No. 170 WORK Brief No. 57	OEK Brief No. 66 WORK Brief No. 61

CHILD DAY-CARE WORKERS

Supervise groups of preschool children, usually while parents are working. May provide learning experiences through stories, games, songs, arts and crafts. Help plan programs and activities.

Day-care centers throughout the country.

Undetermined. Mostly women.

High school necessary; college may be, depending on the center. Training in work with children desirable; teaching certification helpful.

Interest in and liking for children, emotional stability, patience, enthusiasm, cheerfulness.

Want ads; direct application to centers.

May advance to supervisory or administrative positions, depending on education and experience.

Vary widely, typically are not high. In some cases are same as those of teachers in church-supported schools.

Great demand for workers. Several thousand needed each year during 1970s. Men encouraged.

WORK Brief No. 62

CITY MANAGERS

Develop, administer, supervise city government in line with policies set by mayor and council. Appoint, supervise department heads, other employees; see that all laws and ordinances are enforced; prepare annual budget; recommend and develop long-range plans for improvement of services; schedule projects and assign priorities; attend council meetings.

In about 2600 U.S. cities having council-manager form of government.

Close to 3000 persons employed as city managers; few women.

Bachelor's or master's degree in public administration, political science, business administration, or social sciences. Some graduate programs in public administration require internships.

Initiative, good judgment, technical knowledge. Ability to delegate authority, supervise, get along well with people, gain their confidence and understanding; sensitivity to wants and needs of people.

Most persons have some government employment experience before being appointed city manager. Many start as assistant manager in large city. University placement service usually knows of job opportunities; International City Managers' Association can furnish leads.

Most successful city managers are sought by competing cities that offer better salaries or greater challenges. Some find even better administration jobs in other areas of government or in private industry.

About $9000 annually in cities under 5000 population, up to $30,000 in cities with more than 250,000 population.

About 70 cities a year are changing to this form of government. Number of new jobs in city management and similar work is expected to absorb all qualified young men and women available through 1970s.

OEK Brief No. 96
WORK Brief No. 64

CITY PLANNERS

Prepare long-range plans for urban development, taking into account population trends, civic goals, land usage, public facilities, economic factors, and the like. Coordinate efforts with those of civic leaders, agencies, groups. Present plans.

The majority work for government agencies at local, state, or federal level. Some work for private planning agencies, for architectural, engineering, and construction companies, and as consultants.

More than 7000; 5% women.

Minimum requirement: bachelor's degree. Graduate degree in planning or related field needed to start some jobs, and required for advancement.

Analytical, abstract reasoning abilities, intelligence, drive, resourcefulness, vision, good judgment, tact, persuasive and administrative abilities, thoroughness.

Apply direct to planning agencies or to civil service office. Watch openings listed in *Jobs in Planning*, published by American Society of Planning Officials.

Field is expanding rapidly and new jobs are opening regularly. Can become senior planner, director of planning, or work in larger city.

Start: $7500–$10,000, depending on education. Average: roughly from $9500 in small cities to $30,000 or more in largest.

Serious shortage of planners. Best chances to those with graduate degrees.

OEK Brief No. 209
WORK Brief No. 65

OCCUPATION	CLERGYMEN	CLERKS, BOOKSTORE
DUTIES	Attend to spiritual, moral, educational needs of congregation or parish. Conduct worship services, administer rites and sacraments, prepare and deliver sermons. May teach classes in church doctrine; visit and counsel members, others in community; coordinate church activities, handle administration, participate in community activities; study, write, attend meetings.	Sell books, answer customers' questions, take orders, wrap goods, unpack cartons, check invoices, dust and stock shelves. May make window displays, advise book buyer; do typing.
WHERE EMPLOYED	In congregations throughout U.S.; in foreign countries as missionaries; in armed forces, various institutions as chaplains; in theological schools as professors; in area and headquarters offices as administrators.	In bookstores, book sections in department stores and other book outlets throughout the country.
NUMBER OF WORKERS	About 295,000 Protestant ministers, some women; 6500 male rabbis in three branches of Judaism; 60,000 Roman Catholic priests.	Several thousands.
EDUCATION AND TRAINING	College plus at least 3 years in theological seminary. Seminary often includes up to year of practical training under experienced minister. A few denominations require only college or Bible institute.	High school necessary; some college helpful.
SPECIAL QUALIFICATIONS	Deep religious conviction and dedication, superior skill in working with people, wholesome personality, high moral and ethical standards, vigorous and creative mind, capacity to speak and write correctly and convincingly.	Interest in and liking for books; good memory; orderliness; perseverance.
WAYS TO ENTER FIELD	Theology and Bible school graduates are usually placed or assisted by the school in which they studied, or assigned by the headquarters of their denomination or religious order. Some start as assistant pastors.	Want ads, direct application.
CHANCE OF ADVANCEMENT	Move to larger or more affluent congregation; assume administrative responsibility for denomination in geographic area or headquarters; with postgraduate training, some teach in seminaries.	May advance to managerial position.
EARNINGS	Most clergymen earn about $8000. This includes salary, gifts, fees, and value of housing.	Average: $100 a week.
SUPPLY AND DEMAND	Severe shortage of ministers, rabbis, priests. Many churches unable to get full-time clergymen. Not enough graduates for replacements; at same time, many new congregations need clergymen.	New bookstores constantly opening. Need for experienced workers great.
REFERENCES	OEK Brief No. 67 WORK Brief No. 67	OEK Brief No. 113 WORK Brief No. 47

CLERKS, CORRESPONDENCE

Answer routine letters and telephone calls, such as inquiries, complaints, orders, adjustments. Gather information, compose letter or choose form letter. May type letters, dictate to stenographer, use dictating machine.

Organizations having large volume of mail, such as mail-order houses, department stores, government agencies, wholesale supply houses.

Many thousands of men and women.

High school diploma required; some college training preferred. A week to 3 months of on-the-job training usually given.

Writing and clerical ability, initiative, good judgment and memory, tact, courtesy.

Newspaper want ads, state and private employment agencies, civil service offices, direct application. May start as secretary, typist, or junior correspondent.

Limited. Can become section head or correspondence supervisor.

Junior correspondents: $4000–$6300. Experienced: to $7000 or more.

Correspondents increasing as business and industry expand. Many openings for the qualified.

OEK Brief No. 320
WORK Brief No. 76

CLERKS, FILE

File records, correspondence, memos, other material alphabetically, numerically, chronologically, or by other convenient system. Maintain file drawers, look up information, keep files up to date.

Offices of every sizable business, company, organization, institution, and government agency throughout the U.S.

About 170,000; 85% women.

High school recommended. Short period of on-the-job training usually given.

Patience, neatness, attention to details, good memory, reliability, liking for routine.

Want ads, state or private employment agencies, civil service office, or direct application to employers. Summer jobs might provide a good start.

To head file clerk or department supervisor. May become typist, secretary, receptionist, switchboard operator.

Union average: $5200 a year, depending largely on locality. Head file clerk averages about $6000.

Rapid turnover; constant demand. Little competition for beginning positions.

OEK Brief No. 328
WORK Brief No. 123

CLERKS, POSTAL

Window clerks sell stamps, money orders; register, insure mail; compute postage; answer questions. Distribution clerks sort mail, cancel outgoing mail; may operate machines that do this work.

Post offices and railway mail cars.

About 300,000; 22% women.

High school graduates preferred. On-the-job training varies in length.

18 years old, U.S. citizen. Must pass civil service exam. Physical stamina, good memory, accuracy, clerical aptitude. Reliability, adaptability desirable.

Apply to post office or civil service office. May start as substitute, receive permanent status in a year or more.

Limited. Can become supervisor, get more desirable assignment at same pay level.

Start: $3.90 an hour.

Demand expected to increase slightly despite continued automation of post offices. Many openings due to turnover.

OEK Brief No. 18
WORK Brief No. 251

OCCUPATION	CLERKS, SHIPPING AND RECEIVING	CLERKS, STOCK
DUTIES	Prepare merchandise for shipping. May pack, wrap, weigh, label, route packages; open, unpack, inspect, store, or route incoming merchandise; load and unload shipments in trucks or freight cars; use hand or power trucks. Keep records of shipments. May specialize in one or more of these duties.	Arrange and store stock according to a set system, fill orders and requisitions, keep records, take inventory. May type lists and reports, do simple bookkeeping. May specialize in one or more of these duties.
WHERE EMPLOYED	Manufacturing companies, distributors, wholesale and mail-order houses, warehouses, retail stores, and the like. Throughout U.S., but mostly in large cities and industrial areas.	Wherever stocks of material or merchandise are stored. Companies, stores, warehouses, wholesale houses, hospitals, hotels, government agencies, and the like.
NUMBER OF WORKERS	About 380,000; 8% women.	About 500,000 stock clerks and storekeepers; 80% men.
EDUCATION AND TRAINING	High school diploma preferred but not usually required. Some on-the-job training usually given.	High school diploma desirable but not usually required. On-the-job training is usual.
SPECIAL QUALIFICATIONS	Physical strength and stamina often necessary. Legible handwriting, ability to understand and follow instructions, knowledge of arithmetic. May have to be bonded.	Knowledge of arithmetic and spelling, legible handwriting. Orderliness, reliability, good memory helpful. Physical strength and stamina needed for some positions.
WAYS TO ENTER FIELD	Apply direct to employer, watch want ads in newspapers, visit local office of state employment agency.	Newspaper want ads, direct application to employers, state employment agencies are the best ways to find job openings. Take civil service exam for government jobs.
CHANCE OF ADVANCEMENT	Limited. Can become head shipping clerk, warehouse manager, or (with further education) traffic manager.	Fair for those willing to take responsibility. Can become stock supervisor, warehouse manager, chief storekeeper.
EARNINGS	Wage range: $2.60–$3.86 an hour. Supervisors and managers can make more.	Range: $92–$140 a week. Supervisors make more.
SUPPLY AND DEMAND	Demand decreasing slightly because of automated methods of shipping, loading, unloading. Still 12,000 a year; jobs fairly easy to get.	Some increase in number of stock clerks expected. Many openings; little competition for beginning jobs.
REFERENCES	OEK Brief No. 352 WORK Brief No. 295	OEK Brief No. 354 WORK Brief No. 309

COMMERCIAL ARTISTS

Draw or select, letter, lay out, design, and paste up illustrations for publications, displays, advertisements. May create, develop, and sketch ideas for advertisements or designs. May teach, do free-lance work.

Advertising agencies, commercial art studios, publishing and printing companies, mail-order houses, department stores, greeting-card companies, government agencies, schools. Many are self-employed.

About 50,000; 33% women.

High school plus 2 or 3 years in art school or junior college, or college training in commercial art or fine arts.

Artistic ability, good taste, imagination, perseverance, eye for details, adaptability, ability to work under pressure.

Prepare a portfolio of drawings, then apply direct to employers. School placement service, want ads helpful. May start as staff artist, free-lance after gaining experience.

Good for those with talent, ambition. Can become art director, designer, illustrator; free-lance; open own art studio.

Start: $4500–$5000. Experienced: $5000–$10,000. Top: $20,000 or more. Free-lance: $25–$1000 or more for each drawing.

Moderate increase in demand for trained artists. Keen competition for openings and advancement. Best opportunities for women in textile industry and department stores.

OEK Brief No. 65
WORK Brief No. 70

COMPOSITORS

Set type by machine or by hand. By machine, press keys similar to typewriter's; machine duplicates the letters. By hand, select letters needed; assemble in correct order; arrange in galleys and lock into forms.

Newspaper plants, commercial printing companies, book and periodical publishers, and typesetting shops that provide type used by printers. Most work in large cities.

About 180,000 composing-room employees. Some are women.

High school graduation plus 4–6-year apprenticeship required. Trade school training helpful; may learn trade on the job.

Good eyesight, finger dexterity, concentration, accuracy. Knowledge of spelling, grammar, word division.

Apply direct to employer or obtain information regarding openings from union office. Want ads, state employment service may be helpful.

To foreman, plant superintendent, plant manager, printing cost estimator. May open own plant.

Wage range: $3–$5.50 an hour.

Printing industry expanding. Good employment opportunities, but new typesetting methods may gradually limit increase in openings for compositors.

OEK Brief No. 90
WORK Brief No. 72

CONSTRUCTION MACHINERY OPERATORS

Operate heavy machinery: power shovels, cranes, bulldozers, hoists, pile drivers, earth-movers, pumps, concrete mixers, paving machines. May perform minor maintenance and repair jobs on machinery. May specialize in one type of machinery.

Most work for general contractors, especially in heavy construction; others for railroads, public utilities, factories and mines, government public works and highway departments throughout the U.S.

About 310,000, almost all men.

High school desirable plus on-the-job training, technical school, or 3-year formal apprenticeship.

Mechanical aptitude, physical strength and stamina, good vision and coordination. Teamwork and safety consciousness are important.

Most begin as helpers or oilers, an increasing number as apprentices. Apply to contractors, union, or companies that rent heavy equipment.

Learn to operate more complicated machinery and thus increase pay. Can become foreman, superintendent, contractor.

Vary according to machine and location. Crane: $4.70–$8.35. Bulldozer: $3.90–$7.85. Highest earnings go to union power-shovel and crane operators.

Employment rise expected to continue indefinitely. High school graduates will have the best chances for apprenticeships.

OEK Brief No. 285
WORK Brief No. 74

OCCUPATION	COOKS AND CHEFS	COOPERATIVE EXTENSION WORKERS
DUTIES	Prepare and cook food, usually in large quantities. May estimate food consumption, decide on size of portions, help plan menus. May specialize in one kind of food or method of cooking. Chefs supervise all kitchen workers.	Help farm families improve agricultural production and marketing, home management and nutrition through demonstrations, tours, meetings, youth programs, individual assistance. Help solve community problems. Give information and advice through pamphlets, newspapers, magazines, radio, TV, personal contacts.
WHERE EMPLOYED	Restaurants, cafeterias, hotels, clubs, hospitals, schools, department stores, private households.	Mostly county level: Cooperative Extension Service, a joint project of U.S. Department of Agriculture and state land-grant colleges. Rural counties, especially in South and Midwest, employ most.
NUMBER OF WORKERS	670,000 men and women, not including private household cooks.	Over 15,000 in counties, 3300 at state universities, 200–300 in federal service. About ½ these numbers are women.
EDUCATION AND TRAINING	High school diploma preferred, plus vocational or trade school training, apprenticeship, or on-the-job training.	B.S. in agriculture for men, home economics for women. Specialists should have master's degree in agronomy, horticulture, livestock breeding, or the like.
SPECIAL QUALIFICATIONS	Health certificate often required. Cleanliness, physical stamina, ability to work under pressure, keen sense of taste.	Must get along well with people, have leadership and administrative ability. Farm background helpful.
WAYS TO ENTER FIELD	Apply to union or to restaurant or other employer. Want ads, state employment agencies also helpful.	Apply to director of state extension service at state college of agriculture. May find job through college placement bureau.
CHANCE OF ADVANCEMENT	Good. Can specialize, switch to better restaurant, become head cook or chef, open own eating place. Advancement may be slow.	Good. Can become administrator or specialist, or switch to teaching. Graduate degree sometimes required.
EARNINGS	Average: $6300. Experienced cooks and chefs in large restaurants and hotels earn $7500–$15,000 or more. Men make more than women.	Start: $7200. Experienced: $10,500–$15,000. Specialists and administrators may make more.
SUPPLY AND DEMAND	Demand increasing; shortage of well-trained, experienced cooks. Heavy competition for top jobs.	Demand increasing, particularly in depressed rural areas.
REFERENCES	OEK Brief No. 115 WORK Brief No. 75	OEK Brief No. 92 WORK Brief No. 77

CREDIT COLLECTORS

By letters, telephone calls, personal visits attempt to collect overdue bills from debtors. May compose own letters or use form letters; contact elusive debtor's neighbors, co-workers, family in attempt to locate him. If debtor is traced to another town, arrange for assistance of collection agency there. Keep records; may report progress, collections to client.

In credit collection agencies that service retail stores, banks, utility companies, travel agencies, professional people, other clients; credit or accounts-receivable departments of retail, wholesale, manufacturing firms.

30,000 men and women are employed by credit collection agencies.

High school diploma. Business experience and college-level studies are essential for collectors who wish to advance in the field. On-the-job training usually provided.

Aggressiveness, persistence, persuasiveness, imagination, tact, patience, perception, good judge of people, ability to get along well with others.

Credit department of large retail store is ideal entry. Apply direct to stores, wholesale and manufacturing companies, credit collection agencies. Help-wanted ads and state employment service often list credit collector jobs.

May be promoted to collection supervisor, credit collection manager. Sometimes establish own collection agency.

Usually commission, or salary plus commission. Average: $7000–$10,000. Agency managers: $15,000 or more.

There is a need for collectors in every part of the country, mostly in large cities and resort areas. Capable young men and women will find ample opportunity as the credit industry grows at a healthy rate.

OEK Brief No. 91
WORK Brief No. 79

CRIMINOLOGISTS

Study crime and criminals scientifically; seek solutions to problem of crime. May specialize in laws, specific offenses, reactions of society to lawbreaking. Explore theoretical and practical aspects of crime.

In universities, social agencies, police and penal systems, government agencies.

Undetermined.

Bachelor's degree minimum requirement. May major in sociology, psychology, political science, social work. Master's degree necessary for teaching, research, penology.

Analytical ability, emotional stability, inquiring mind. Interest in and concern for society.

College placement service, direct application, professional journals.

In teaching, may advance to full professorship. In other areas, may advance to administrative positions.

Teachers average $10,000–$12,000 a year; administrators, $15,000–$35,000.

Shortage of trained workers.

OEK Brief No. 385
WORK Brief No. 80

DANCERS

Perform on stage, screen, television; in chorus, group, or solo; in classical ballet or modern dance, in dance adaptations for musical shows, in folk dances, or in tap and other popular dance forms. May combine teaching with stage work, or teach full time in universities or other schools of dance. May provide dance therapy in treatment of mental patients.

Most professional employment in New York, Chicago, Dallas, Washington, San Francisco, Los Angeles, Miami, Las Vegas. Teach in large cities throughout U.S., in schools of dance and universities.

23,000; half are dancing teachers. 80% of all dancers are women. In ballet and modern, as many men as women.

Begin serious training by age 12. Typical professional training: 10-12 lessons a week plus practice. Most dancers have professional audition by age 17 or 18. College education an advantage for teaching.

Unusual talent and intense desire to become good dancer. Determination, perseverance, patience. Excellent health, unusual physical vitality, agility; good feet with normal arches; well-formed body with good muscular control; physical grace.

Auditions, which are publicized through union notices, newspapers, trade papers, booking agencies, and the call boards of professional schools; booking agencies. Some start in summer theater, community productions, road-company musicals.

Develop specialty number as soloist; understudy principal roles, become choreographer or teacher; open own school of dance. Most would like to gain stardom, but few make it.

Rehearsal pay $135 a week; performance, $155 a week minimum for group members.

Teaching outlook far brighter than performing. Supply of trained dancers has for many years exceeded the demand, so competition is terrific. Men dancers face less competition than women.

OEK Brief No. 150
WORK Brief No. 85

OCCUPATION	DENTAL ASSISTANTS	DENTAL HYGIENISTS
DUTIES	Give chairside assistance to dentist: settle patient in dental chair, hand supplies and instruments to dentist, sterilize instruments. May operate X-ray machine, develop and mount X rays, mix filling materials and dental cement, perform laboratory procedures. Greet patients, answer telephone, schedule appointments, and handle other office routines.	Clean and polish patients' teeth and massage gums, provide information on proper mouth care. May take and develop X rays for dentist's diagnosis, assist him at chair, perform certain laboratory work, some office duties. Educate public. Teach.
WHERE EMPLOYED	About 90% work for dentists in private practice; others in Public Health Service and Veterans Administration hospitals, local public health departments, private clinics, armed forces.	Usually in private dental offices. Also in health agencies, public schools, armed forces, industry, schools of dental hygiene. Principally in metropolitan areas.
NUMBER OF WORKERS	About 91,000. Except for small number in armed forces, most are women.	About 16,000, mostly women. Some work only part time.
EDUCATION AND TRAINING	High school diploma. Many are trained by dentist for whom they work. Trend toward formal training of 9–24 months in junior college, commercial school, correspondence course, for certification.	High school graduation plus 2 years training in school of dental hygiene, or 4-year degree program.
SPECIAL QUALIFICATIONS	Alertness and quickness; calm, even temperament; discretion; tact; sound judgment; good grooming; ability to be on feet quite a bit of time; ability to put apprehensive patients at ease.	Pass state board exam to obtain license. Excellent finger dexterity and eye-hand coordination, depth perception, and full use of both hands. Pleasing personality.
WAYS TO ENTER FIELD	Schools usually have placement service. Apply direct to dentists; get leads from family dentist, local dental society, dental schools. Check state employment service, want ads, state and federal civil service commissions.	Dental hygiene school placement offices, associations; state, medical, or commercial employment agencies; newspaper want ads; civil service office; school board.
CHANCE OF ADVANCEMENT	Limited. Advancement usually in form of more responsibility and more pay. In other than dental-office employment, may advance to supervisory post.	Limited. With additional training, may become teacher or director in a department of dental hygiene, work in dental health education.
EARNINGS	$3900–$7800, depending on training, experience, location.	Average starting salary: $6000–$8000, depending on education.
SUPPLY AND DEMAND	Excellent outlook, and demand expected to continue increasing. High turnover because of young women who leave to marry.	Workers are much in demand; not nearly enough graduates to fill jobs. About 3100 openings each year.
REFERENCES	OEK Brief No. 272 WORK Brief No. 86	OEK Brief No. 38 WORK Brief No. 87

DENTISTS	DESIGNERS, FASHION	DESIGNERS, INDUSTRIAL
Prevent, diagnose, and correct tooth and gum disorders. Fill cavities, clean teeth, take X rays, extract teeth, take impressions for dentures, advise patients about oral hygiene. May specialize, teach, do lab work.	Design garments: sketch design; may drape, cut, fit, sew fabric, make pattern and sample garment, or supervise others in these steps; choose colors and fabrics; estimate production costs. Usually specialize in one kind of clothing.	Design products to combine attractiveness and functionality at competitive price. Study development of product, competing designs, use, ease of manufacture, cost, durability, public taste.
The great majority are in private practice. About 10% are salaried, working in government agencies, hospitals, clinics, research laboratories, and dental schools.	Clothing manufacturers and wholesalers, stores and shops that sell custom-made clothing, design salons, motion picture and TV studios. Mostly in fashion centers such as New York, Los Angeles, Dallas.	Primarily with large manufacturing companies, design consulting firms, architects, interior designers. May also free-lance, be self-employed as consultants.
103,000 licensed dentists, including teachers and administrators; 2% women.	About 1500 designers and assistants in women's and men's fashions. Most are women.	About 10,000.
2 or 3 years college plus 4 years dental school. 2 or 3 years of postgraduate work needed to specialize.	High school plus 2 or 3 years of fashion design in trade school, art institute, junior college. College degree preferred.	3–5 years of industrial design in art school, university, or technical college. Engineers and architects may qualify.
Scientific interests and aptitude, manual dexterity, spatial perception, business sense, tact, imperturbability. Must pass exam for dental school, state license.	Artistic ability, imagination, interest in fashion, good taste, spatial perception, manual dexterity, stamina, ability to work under pressure.	Creativity, ability to give visible form to ideas, mechanical ability, business sense, understanding of consumer trends, knowledge of form and color.
May work for an established dentist, buy a dentist's practice, or start own practice. Watch dental journals for openings in salaried positions.	School placement services, want ads in clothing trade magazines, direct application. May start as helper, assistant, sketcher, patternmaker.	Apply to industrial design firm or manufacturing company. Begin as assistant, doing more drafting than designing. School placement services may list openings.
Mostly by making reputation and building list of regular patients. Can become specialist, administrator.	Good for those with talent. Can increase earnings by getting better job or opening own salon, store, or clothing company. May free-lance.	Excellent. May become chief designer, start own practice.
Average for all dentists in private practice: about $29,600.	Start: about $6000 a year. Experienced: $8000–$50,000 or more. Top: $100,000 or more.	Beginners: $6500–$7800 a year. Experienced: $8000–$14,000. A few earn up to $25,000 in salaried employment, to $200,000 self-employed.
Shortage of dentists expected to increase with population. Keen competition for admission to dental school.	Some increase in employment expected. Keen competition for jobs at all levels.	Expect moderate increase in employment of designers as more manufacturers see relation between design and sales.
OEK Brief No. 68 WORK Brief No. 89	OEK Brief No. 142 WORK Brief No. 120	OEK Brief No. 7 WORK Brief No. 161

OCCUPATION	DETECTIVES	DIETITIANS
DUTIES	Police officers: investigate crime by tracking suspects, seeking clues, interviewing potential witnesses, observing evidence, working as part of law-enforcement team. Private detectives or operatives: protect property by detecting shoplifters, trespassers, bad-check passers, other offenders; investigate fraudulent claims; trace missing persons, shadow suspects.	Plan diets and menus, supervise food preparation and service, manage and administer food-service activities, teach dietetics and nutrition, counsel clients regarding proper nutrition, do dietary research.
WHERE EMPLOYED	City police departments. As operatives with detective agencies, department stores, hotels, industrial organizations, railroads.	About half work in hospitals. Others are with hotels and restaurants, schools, colleges, government agencies, transportation companies, industrial or company cafeterias, and food manufacturers.
NUMBER OF WORKERS	330,000 police, of whom some are assigned specifically to investigative work. Unknown number of private detectives.	About 30,000; 1% men.
EDUCATION AND TRAINING	High school graduation. Most applicants have 1 or 2 years of college. On police force, pass exam for detective job; then several weeks to several months of training. Operatives usually learn on the job.	College degree in nutrition or institution management. For professional recognition, must also have 1-year internship or 3 years experience.
SPECIAL QUALIFICATIONS	Initiative, good judgment, ability to accept responsibility, mental alertness, good memory, good reasoning powers, patience, perseverance, physical courage. Usually required to drive car.	Interest in and aptitude for science, ability to give and take orders, pleasant personality, administrative ability.
WAYS TO ENTER FIELD	For police jobs, get on the force; take promotional exam for detective. For private detective jobs, apply direct to detective agencies, department stores, large hotels, other organizations.	College placement services helpful. Watch want ads, apply to employers or civil service offices.
CHANCE OF ADVANCEMENT	Based almost entirely on ability to produce results. On police force, may become chief of detectives, department head.	Good chance to attain administrative or supervisory position.
EARNINGS	Police detectives: $8500–$10,000.	Start: $9000. Experienced: $9500–$30,000 or more. May also receive room, board, laundry services.
SUPPLY AND DEMAND	In police work, there is almost no opportunity to start as a detective, for these workers are usually mature policemen who are promoted. Demand for detectives is greater in large cities than in small.	Growing occupation. Need 2000 new graduates a year. Shortage of dietitians; very little competition for openings. Men encouraged.
REFERENCES	OEK Brief No. 274 WORK Brief No. 91	OEK Brief No. 71 WORK Brief No. 93

DISC JOCKEYS

Select and play records; keep up entertaining or interesting line of chatter, much of it ad lib; interview guests; read commercials. May read news, write commercials, make and receive phone calls on the air, operate turntable and controls.

In 5500 radio stations throughout U.S. Some TV stations also employ disc jockeys.

Indeterminate number; very few women.

College degree not absolutely necessary, but advisable. An alternative might be courses at specialized schools of broadcasting located in some large cities.

Self-confidence, outgoing personality, quick wit, tact. Read, talk well in pleasing voice, no strong regional accent or annoying speech habits; vocabulary, grammar above average. Have Federal Communications Commission radio operator's license.

Apply to radio and TV stations for any job; most disc jockeys start at something else, particularly announcing. College placement service can usually help place graduates. May have to audition.

Move to larger station, perhaps as announcer waiting opportunity to become disc jockey. May get more or better time, offers to do other shows, make personal appearances. May move into administrative work in communications.

Nationwide average: $8000. Range goes up to $100,000 earned by a few top stars at large metropolitan stations.

Field is not expanding and the competition is fierce.

OEK Brief No. 296
WORK Brief No. 94

DISPLAY WORKERS

Conceive, design, and create eye-catching and sales-stimulating displays for store windows, counters, walls. May make detailed sketches, make or obtain props, assign and coordinate carpentry, electrical and mechanical work, artistic efforts. May coordinate displays and decorations throughout store for special events.

Retail stores, especially large department stores, employ greatest number. Others work for display-building companies, manufacturers who mass-produce displays for their customers, manufacturers of display fixtures and props.

About 55,000 full-time workers. 35%–40% women, who work as artists, designers, sign makers, painters, mannequin dressers.

High school graduation. Some college training usually preferred; preparation may be in art school. Informal on-the-job training lasts 3–5 years.

Interest and talent in design and art; resourcefulness; imagination, creative ability. Must be practical enough to meet deadlines and stay within budgets.

Apply to stores, display builders. College or art school placement services offer leads. Newspaper ads and state employment service can be helpful.

May specialize in one area of display work, become designer, display director. Some become stage designers, set up own business, occasionally become sales or merchandising executives.

Helpers without college training: $4000–$4500. Designers in training: $4500–$5500. Experienced: $8000 and up. Directors: $10,000 and up.

Employment prospects good and expected to improve. College training becoming a must.

OEK Brief No. 40
WORK Brief No. 95

DRAFTSMEN

Prepare accurate, detailed plans and drawings of machinery, structures, manufactured products. Work from notes and sketches furnished by engineers, architects, designers. Make calculations, write specifications. Usually specialize.

Manufacturing companies, architectural and engineering firms, construction companies, government agencies, public utilities.

About 275,000 draftsmen; 6% women.

High school plus technical school, junior college, trade or correspondence school, or 3- or 4-year apprenticeship.

Good eyesight, liking for detail, accuracy, spatial and mechanical aptitude, ability to concentrate, patience.

Watch want ads in newspapers, technical journals. Employment agencies, placement services of colleges and technical schools, civil service offices.

Limited. With skill and experience can become senior draftsman, designer, chief draftsman.

Start: $4800–$5500. Experienced: $7000–$12,000 or more.

Continued expansion expected due to increasingly complex design problems. Need 16,000 new draftsmen each year.

OEK Brief No. 33
WORK Brief No. 96

OCCUPATION	DRESSMAKERS	DRIVING INSTRUCTORS
DUTIES	Help customer select fabric and design; cut material to pattern; cut and baste; fit and alter; sew, finish garment. May design ladies' clothing; specialize in fitting, alterations; teach dressmaking.	Teach driving skills, traffic laws and regulations, safety practices. Using automobile with dual brakes, teach students to use gearshift or automatic control, brakes; to start, steer, turn, park car. Emphasize caution and safety habits.
WHERE EMPLOYED	Ladies' clothing and department stores, custom dressmaking shops, garment factories, fashion salons, dressmaking schools. Some work at home.	High schools and 2500 commercial driver-training schools throughout U.S.
NUMBER OF WORKERS	About 125,000; 3% men.	About 15,000; a few women.
EDUCATION AND TRAINING	High school preferred, plus trade school and 2–4 years of on-the-job training.	High school diploma minimum for commercial driving instructors; college degree in education for high school teachers.
SPECIAL QUALIFICATIONS	Manual dexterity, sewing skill, good eyesight, accuracy, neatness, patience; color discrimination, sense of form, spatial perception.	Regular or special driver's license, expert driving ability, good driving record, patience, pleasant personality, good judgment, calm temperament, neat appearance.
WAYS TO ENTER FIELD	Apply direct to employers. Trade school placement service, union, state employment service may help. May start as hand sewer, seamstress, assistant.	Apply to commercial driving school or (with teacher's certificate) to high school. Start as an instructor trainee.
CHANCE OF ADVANCEMENT	Can become custom dressmaker, designer; start own business.	Fair. Can become supervisor, manager; open own school.
EARNINGS	Custom dressmakers; $1.50–$5 an hour or more.	Average: $7800.
SUPPLY AND DEMAND	Trend downward for custom dressmakers and for fitters, alterations women, seamstresses.	Demand growing for formal driver education. Number of instructors expected to increase rapidly.
REFERENCES	OEK Brief No. 24 WORK Brief No. 97	OEK Brief No. 324 WORK Brief No. 98

DRYCLEANING WORKERS

Mark and sort garments; operate cleaning machines, extractors, dryers; remove spots and stains; make needed repairs; press garments; inspect and bag garments. Usually specialize in one of these duties.

Retail and wholesale drycleaning plants.

About 225,000 laundry and drycleaning operators, men and women.

High school diploma preferred. On-the-job training for skilled positions may last 6 months to 3 years.

Good eyesight and color vision, manual dexterity, thoroughness, good health.

Apply to drycleaning plant. Usually start as a helper.

Good chance to become skilled worker such as spotter, presser, drycleaner. Can become plant manager; start own business.

Average: $1.56 an hour for women; $2.05 for men.

Industry is growing. High turnover among women. Skilled workers needed.

OEK Brief No. 59
WORK Brief No. 101

ECOLOGISTS

Study the relation of plants, animals, microorganisms to each other and to their environment. May work in related professions: agronomy, entomology, horticulture, oceanography. May work in environmental technology: operate sewage plant, inspect sanitation facilities, work in public health lab.

In universities, state and local health departments, government agencies, industries, municipal sanitary districts.

About 4300 professional ecologists.

College degree necessary; postgraduate work essential for advancement. (For semiskilled technologists, high school usually necessary.)

Scientific interest and aptitude. Keen interest in environment; curiosity, ingenuity, perseverance, analytical ability.

Personal recommendation of professor or through college placement bureau, professional journals, want ads, civil service exam.

Good and varied. Usually means more pay, more responsibility. May become head of project or department in research, teaching, or industry.

Generally high. Teachers, government workers start at about $10,000. In industry, usually more.

About 12,000 professionals needed by 1980. Also thousands of jobs for semiskilled throughout the 1970's.

OEK Brief No. 250
WORK Brief No. 102

ECONOMISTS

Study conditions affecting production, distribution, consumption of goods and services. May specialize in fiscal, labor, agricultural, industrial, social economics. Compile and analyze data, teach, do research, serve as consultants.

Colleges and universities; government agencies; banks and insurance companies; business, trade, and industrial organizations; research associations. A few are self-employed as consultants.

About 33,000; 15% women.

Bachelor's degree in economics the minimum; graduate degree required for teaching and research, top jobs in all fields.

Aptitude for math, abstract reasoning ability, high level of intelligence, accuracy, ability to concentrate, persistence.

Recommendation of college professor. College placement service, notices in professional journals. Direct application to employers, civil service offices.

Excellent for those with graduate degree. Can become administrator, executive, consultant, professor.

Teaching: average $18,000. Business: average $20,000. Government: $14,000–$23,000. May also earn royalties, consulting fees.

Demand growing rapidly, especially in teaching. Best chances for those with Ph.D.

OEK Brief No. 79
WORK Brief No. 103

OCCUPATION	EDITORS, BOOK	EDITORS, MAGAZINE
DUTIES	Read, select manuscripts; suggest revisions; reorganize, rewrite for clarity and style; check for accuracy, consistency; help select illustrations, format. May see book through production. May specialize in one kind of book.	Choose stories, articles, poems, artwork determine format and arrangement. May write editorials, features, articles; edit, rewrite articles; suggest changes to authors; solicit manuscripts. Plan future issues; supervise staff.
WHERE EMPLOYED	Over 600 publishers of trade, technical, educational, scholarly, and reference books. Mostly in publishing centers such as New York, Chicago, Boston, Philadelphia, Los Angeles.	Publishing companies, trade and professional associations, business and industrial companies. There are more than 30,000 popular opinion, news, trade, technical, religious professional, literary, and company magazines
NUMBER OF WORKERS	Undetermined.	At least 30,000, plus many assistants and associates.
EDUCATION AND TRAINING	College degree essential for most jobs. Master's or Ph.D. helpful for advancement, especially in technical, educational publishing.	College degree essential in most cases. English and journalism majors usually preferred.
SPECIAL QUALIFICATIONS	Literary interests and aptitudes, ability to abstract and organize ideas, verbal reasoning ability, critical judgment, tact, accuracy, ability to concentrate well.	Literary interests and aptitudes, skill with the written word, administrative ability critical judgment, accuracy, ability to work under pressure.
WAYS TO ENTER FIELD	Watch want ads in newspapers, trade magazines; use college placement service or commercial employment agencies that specialize in publishing jobs; apply direct to publishing companies. May start as editorial assistant or secretary.	Watch want ads in newspapers, trade journals; apply to magazine publishers. May start as editorial assistant, researcher, secretary
CHANCE OF ADVANCEMENT	Can become senior editor, managing editor, publishing executive. Some free-lance.	Limited. In large publishing companies can become executive, but editor is top position on most magazines.
EARNINGS	Editorial assistants: $4900–$7800. Editors: $7500–$15,000. Top: $20,000 or more.	Start: $5200 a year. Experienced: $8000–$10,000. Top: $25,000 or more.
SUPPLY AND DEMAND	Demand increasing in educational, paperback publishing. Considerable competition for advancement.	Special-interest magazines increasing. Competition is stiff for beginning and top jobs Well-qualified editorial people always in demand.
REFERENCES	OEK Brief No. 355 WORK Brief No. 44	OEK Brief No. 245 WORK Brief No. 196

EDITORS, NEWSPAPER	ELECTRICIANS, CONSTRUCTION	ELECTRICIANS, MAINTENANCE
Give assignments to reporters; evaluate stories. May write articles and editorials, edit copy, make up or supervise makeup of pages. Variety of tasks depends on size of paper.	Install wiring, fixtures, and electrical equipment in buildings being built or remodeled. Install conduit, pull wire through, connect to components, test. Follow blueprints and specifications. Use hand and power tools, test equipment.	Maintain and repair electrical systems, machinery, and equipment; may modify and install electrical equipment. Make periodic maintenance inspections and tests, locate sources of trouble, repair or replace faulty parts. Use hand and power tools, test equipment.
On large and small newspapers throughout the country.	Electrical contractors, government agencies, large industrial or business companies. Many are self-employed.	Manufacturing plants, government agencies, public utilities, mines, institutions, large retail and wholesale establishments, other large organizations.
Undetermined.	Approximately 190,000; less than 1% women.	About 250,000; less than 1% women.
College degree in journalism or liberal arts.	High school plus 4-year apprenticeship or longer period of on-the-job training.	High school plus 4-year apprenticeship or on-the-job training. Trade and technical school training helpful.
Curiosity, perseverance, good judgment, ability to get along with many different types of people, integrity.	Mechanical aptitude, ability in basic math, manual dexterity, accuracy, alertness, reliability. In some areas, may have to pass test to get local license.	May have to pass test for local license. Mechanical aptitude, ability in math, manual dexterity, reliability, accuracy, alertness.
College placement bureaus, employment agencies, want ads in newspapers and professional publications, direct application.	Apply to union or contractor, other employers; see state employment service.	Apply to factories, other employers, or civil service offices. Watch newspaper ads. State employment service may be of help.
Editor is usually a top job. On large newspapers may work up to editor in chief. May start own newspaper, with good supply of capital.	Can become foreman, superintendent, estimator, free lance; start own contracting business.	Some chance to become foreman, chief electrician, maintenance supervisor. Can switch to construction electrician.
Rates for jobs leading to editor often set by contracts with The Newspaper Guild. Beginning reporters: $100–$135 a week. Experienced: about $160–$250 or more. Editors: to $50,000.	Average union wage: $6.82 an hour minimum. Apprentices start at 40%–50% of journeyman wage.	Journeymen: $3.07–$5.29 an hour. Apprentices start at 40%–50% of journeyman wage.
Good future on small-town or suburban area papers. Opportunities also for those who are specialists in economics, science, and the like.	Considerable interest expected, owing to increased use of electrical equipment. Keen competition for apprenticeships.	Automation of plants and offices means more jobs for maintenance electricians. Gradual increase expected.
OEK Brief No. 69 WORK Brief No. 217	OEK Brief No. 25 WORK Brief No. 106	OEK Brief No. 25 WORK Brief No. 106

OCCUPATION	ELECTRONIC DATA-PROCESSING MACHINE OPERATORS	ELECTROPLATERS
DUTIES	Operate computers or auxiliary data-processing machines: set machine to perform operation desired, feed in punched cards or tapes, watch for errors, pass data to next machine in the system. May wire simple plugboards.	Use electrochemical process to plate metal articles. Following specifications, mix chemical solution, calculate current and time required. Prepare articles, immerse, time, remove, rinse, dry. Check finished items for defects. May polish with lathe, abrasive belt, or pressure blasting; may apply lacquer.
WHERE EMPLOYED	Organizations that have data-processing installations, such as government agencies, insurance companies, banks, manufacturing companies, large retail stores, public utilities, data-processing centers.	Independent electroplating job shops and plating departments of manufacturing plants. Mostly in industrial states, especially in and around metalworking centers.
NUMBER OF WORKERS	About 200,000 console and auxiliary equipment operators, men and women.	About 17,000 men.
EDUCATION AND TRAINING	High school diploma essential. Some college or business school training preferred. On-the-job training takes 1–6 months.	High school graduation, plus 3 or 4 years of on-the-job training or 3-year formal apprenticeship. Apprentice applicants must be at least 18.
SPECIAL QUALIFICATIONS	Clerical and mathematical ability, manual dexterity, some mechanical ability, alertness, accuracy, ability to work under pressure.	Exactness, eye for details, patience, dependability, manual dexterity, good eye-hand-arm coordination.
WAYS TO ENTER FIELD	Apply to company with a data-processing installation. Newspaper want ads, school placement services, employment agencies helpful. Take civil service exam for government jobs.	Apply to electroplating shops and metalworking plants. Contact union office. Watch want ads; visit state employment service office.
CHANCE OF ADVANCEMENT	Good chance to become supervisor or (with more training) programmer, systems analyst.	Limited. Can become foreman or open own electroplating shop.
EARNINGS	Beginners: $113–$122 a week. Experienced: to $200. Top: to $365.	Skilled men: $1.75–$3.50 an hour. Top: $13,000 a year.
SUPPLY AND DEMAND	Demand increasing rapidly, especially for trained computer operators. Competition for jobs is growing.	Demand increasing somewhat. More training and skill may be required in the future. Apprenticeships scarce.
REFERENCES	OEK Brief No. 322 WORK Brief No. 107	OEK Brief No. 311 WORK Brief No. 111

ELEVATOR CONSTRUCTORS	EMPLOYMENT COUNSELORS	ENGINEERS, AEROSPACE
Assemble and install elevators, escalators, dumbwaiters, and similar equipment. Do careful adjusting, testing, inspecting of entire assembly.	Learn of applicant's abilities, experience, interests, preferences, and needs through application form and interview. Try to direct applicant to suitable job. May check references, administer and score aptitude and interest tests. May develop vocational plan for client with team of specialists.	Plan, design, develop, test, supervise production of aircraft, missiles, rockets. May specialize in one type of product or one area of work. May teach aeronautical engineering.
Companies that install or maintain elevators and similar equipment; government elevator-licensing agencies.	Private and state employment agencies.	Manufacturers of aircraft and spacecraft frames, engines, components; government agencies; airlines; colleges and universities.
About 15,000 men.	About 6000 in state employment offices; 2000 in private or community agencies.	More than 60,000; some women.
High school education, plus at least two years of continuous job experience, including 6 months on-the-job training at the factory of a major elevator firm.	At least a bachelor's degree; master's degree preferred. In-service training.	At least bachelor's degree in aeronautical engineering. For research work and technical specialties, graduate degree desirable.
Must have working knowledge of electricity, electronics, hydraulics; mechanical aptitude.	Ability to deal with people, work without direct or imposed supervision. Emotional stability, tact, persuasiveness.	Ability, interest in science and math. Logical mind, persistence in detail work. For some jobs, engineers must pass state exam for professional engineer's license.
Direct application to elevator company; want ads; employment agencies; union office.	Apply direct to private agencies or watch want ads for openings. For public agency, apply direct and, if qualified, take civil service exam.	Campus interviews with company representatives, college placement bureaus, direct application, want ads, notices in engineering journals.
May advance to foreman, construction superintendent, with more education and experience.	In public agencies, advance by passing exams. Top, state supervisor. In private firms, may specialize or open own agency.	Chances good for advancement to chief engineer, project director, executive positions.
Average union minimum: $6.65 an hour. Helpers are usually paid at a rate of 70% of the craftsman's pay.	Trainees: $6500 a year. Experienced: to $15,000.	Starting average: $10,200. Salaries higher in industry, lower in government and teaching.
Expect about 6000 job openings annually through the 1970s.	The demand should increase, especially for those with advanced degrees. Expect 1100 openings a year.	Demand fluctuates periodically because of changes in defense expenditures; however, job opportunities are expected to be favorable.
WORK Brief No. 112	OEK Brief No. 325 WORK Brief No. 113	OEK Brief No. 201 WORK Brief No. 6

OCCUPATION	ENGINEERS, AGRICULTURAL	ENGINEERS, AIR-CONDITIONING AND REFRIGERATION
DUTIES	Apply scientific and engineering principles to agricultural problems in the areas of farm machinery and processing equipment, farm buildings, electric power, soil and water conservation.	Design, develop, test, plan, and supervise production of air-conditioning and refrigeration equipment. May sell equipment, oversee installation and service, adapt systems to customers' needs. May serve as consultants to manufacturers, contractors.
WHERE EMPLOYED	More than half work in private industry—for farm equipment manufacturers and dealers, electric power companies, financial institutions; others for federal and state government agencies. Throughout U.S. and abroad.	Air-conditioning manufacturers, dealers, distributors; technical schools, colleges, and universities; contractors; food, dairy plants; government. Consultants may be self-employed.
NUMBER OF WORKERS	About 13,000; some women.	Undetermined. About 220,000 mechanical engineers.
EDUCATION AND TRAINING	At least bachelor's degree in agricultural, mechanical, electrical, or civil engineering. Graduate degree desirable.	Bachelor's degree in mechanical engineering. For research and top jobs, graduate degree often required.
SPECIAL QUALIFICATIONS	Ability, interest in science and math. Mechanical ability. Farm background helpful. For some jobs a state licensing exam must be passed.	Ability in science and math; mechanical interests and aptitude; logical, systematic mind. In some jobs, may have to take exam for state license.
WAYS TO ENTER FIELD	Campus interviews with company representatives, college placement bureaus, want ads in newspapers and professional journals, direct application, civil service offices.	Campus interviews, college placement bureaus, direct application, employment agencies, want ads.
CHANCE OF ADVANCEMENT	Good for qualified workers. May advance to supervisory positions in sales, teaching, research.	Good. Can advance to chief engineer, supervisory and executive positions. Can start own business as a consultant or contractor.
EARNINGS	Starting average: $10,000.	Start: $10,100–$11,400. Experienced: $13,000–$18,000. Top: $25,000 or more.
SUPPLY AND DEMAND	Demand increasing rapidly. Greatest need for engineers with graduate degree for teaching and research.	Air-conditioning industry growing rapidly; demand for trained engineers exceeds supply.
REFERENCES	OEK Brief No. 202 WORK Brief No. 7	OEK Brief No. 253 WORK Brief No. 8

ENGINEERS, CERAMIC

Supervise mining, production of ceramic materials; design, develop, test, sell, service ceramic products. May specialize in glass, refractories, whitewares, porcelain, enamel, abrasives, structural clay products. May teach, do research.

Most work for manufacturing companies in the ceramic industry, especially in industrial states such as New York, California, Texas, Ohio, Pennsylvania; a few for the government and in universities.

About 10,000; some women.

Bachelor's degree in ceramic engineering is the minimum. Graduate degree required for independent research.

Aptitude and interest in math and science, mechanical aptitude, reasoning ability, persistence, ingenuity. May need state license.

On-campus interviews, college placement bureau, notices in professional publications, newspaper want ads.

Good chances for ambitious, energetic men. Can become director of research project, production manager, administrator.

Start: $700–$800 a month. Experienced: $11,000–$15,000 a year. Top: $25,000 or more.

Demand increasing in this small but rapidly growing profession. Every year there are about 400 openings, more than there are qualified graduates.

OEK Brief No. 204
WORK Brief No. 58

ENGINEERS, CHEMICAL

Apply principles of chemistry and engineering to production and processing operations. Using knowledge of basic chemical research, determine production methods, design plant and equipment, schedule construction, oversee operations.

Most work for manufacturing companies, especially in the chemical, drug, and petroleum industries. Others work for government agencies, colleges and universities, or are self-employed as consultants.

More than 50,000; a few women.

Bachelor's degree essential. Master's or doctor's helpful for all positions, required for some research and teaching positions.

Interest in and aptitude for science and math, mechanical aptitude, business sense, reliability, persistence. May need state license.

On-campus interviews, college placement bureau, want ads in newspapers and technical journals, employment agencies.

Excellent. Can become production manager, research director, administrator. About 10% of positions in administration.

Start: $9500–$15,000, depending on education. Experienced: $17,000 or more. Highest salaries in industry, lowest in teaching.

Demand increasing more rapidly than number of graduates. Some competition for top jobs.

OEK Brief No. 1
WORK Brief No. 59

ENGINEERS, CIVIL

Plan, design, supervise construction of roads, tunnels, dams, bridges, airports, railroads, reservoirs, sewage systems, large buildings. Write specifications, prepare cost estimates, inspect and test construction work.

Government agencies, construction companies, transportation companies, engineering and architectural firms, public utilities, and industries such as oil and steel, in U.S. and abroad.

More than 200,000, almost all men.

At least bachelor's degree in civil engineering. Graduate degree helpful for jobs in design, teaching, research.

Aptitude for and interest in physics, math. Some mechanical aptitude, imagination. Thoroughness, persistence, good judgment. May need state license.

On-campus interviews, college placement service, want ads in newspapers, notices in technical journals, civil service offices.

Excellent. Can become superintendent, consultant, executive, or administrator.

Start: $10,000–$11,500. Top: $40,000–$60,000.

Increased demand due to federal and state spending for public construction. Some competition for openings, promotions.

OEK Brief No. 2
WORK Brief No. 66

OCCUPATION	ENGINEERS, ELECTRICAL	ENGINEERS, INDUSTRIAL
DUTIES	Design, develop, supervise production and operation of electrical and electronic equipment. May specialize in electronics or electrical equipment, telephone and telegraph, power, illumination, transportation; teach, do research.	Develop, improve, and set up work systems of men, materials, and equipment. Concerned with saving money or time through efficiency of production methods, materials handling, standards, plant layout, costs, job analysis, safety.
WHERE EMPLOYED	Most work in industry, especially for manufacturers of electrical and electronic equipment, and for public utilities. Others work in colleges and universities, government agencies, engineering firms.	Most work for large manufacturing companies; others for construction and mining companies, public utilities, government agencies, banks and insurance companies, colleges and universities, consulting firms.
NUMBER OF WORKERS	About 230,000 – the largest engineering specialty.	Estimated at 125,000; 3% women.
EDUCATION AND TRAINING	College degree required. Graduate degree helpful, and required for teaching and research.	College degree, preferably in industrial engineering. Courses in business, human relations, math, as well as engineering.
SPECIAL QUALIFICATIONS	Scientific, mathematical, mechanical interests and aptitudes. Logical mind, reliability, good judgment, perseverance. May need state license.	Aptitude for math and science, logical mind, interest in business practices and manufacturing processes, ability to communicate clearly, practicality.
WAYS TO ENTER FIELD	College placement services, want ads in newspapers, notices in technical journals, direct application. May get first job through on-campus interview.	Work-study programs, on-campus job interviews, college placement bureaus, want ads in newspapers and journals, public and private employment agencies.
CHANCE OF ADVANCEMENT	Excellent chance to become manager, executive, consultant.	May advance to supervisory or administrative position, become consultant, start own company.
EARNINGS	Start: $10,500. Experienced: $15,000–$20,000. Top: $40,000 or more.	Starting average: $10,000.
SUPPLY AND DEMAND	Demand increasing in all fields of employment. Not enough engineering graduates to fill the 14,000 job openings annually.	Demand far exceeds the supply. At least 8000 job openings a year.
REFERENCES	OEK Brief No. 3 WORK Brief No. 105	OEK Brief No. 205 WORK Brief No. 162

ENGINEERS, MECHANICAL

Design machines and mechanical equipment. May direct testing, manufacture, installation, operation. May work in research and development, sales, technical writing, administration, consulting, teaching.

Factories, power plants, construction projects, shipyards, military establishments, government agencies, colleges and universities, consulting firms. Mostly in industrial areas.

About 215,000; many women.

Bachelor's degree in mechanical engineering the minimum. May do specialized graduate work.

Aptitude for math and science, interest in mechanics. Should be creative, logical, and systematic, have manual dexterity. May need state license.

College placement offices; want ads in professional journals, trade magazines, newspapers; direct application to employers. Usually recruited while still in college.

Good. Can specialize, become administrator, start own consulting firm.

Start: $800–$1400 a month, depending on education. Top: $20,000 or more a year. A few earn over $100,000 a year.

The demand is great and expected to continue. Not much competition, especially for those with an advanced degree.

OEK Brief No. 4
WORK Brief No. 202

ENGINEERS, METALLURGICAL

Determine methods to concentrate, enrich, and purify ores; reduce concentrated ores to produce metals; do research to obtain physical properties desired such as hardness, proper internal structure, strength, resistance to corrosion.

About half in iron and steel industries; others in nonferrous metal production, fuels, mining, aerospace, atomic energy; a few in private and government labs, colleges and universities, consulting firms.

About 10,000, almost all men.

A B.S. is the usual minimum requirement. Graduate degree often required for high-level positions.

Above-average interest in and aptitude for chemistry, math, and physics. Mechanical aptitude, inquiring mind, accuracy. May need state license.

College placement offices, professional societies, newspaper and trade magazine want ads, state and private employment agencies, direct application.

Excellent. To senior engineer, chief engineer, director of research, administrative positions.

Average starting salary about $10,000.

At least 500 job openings a year. Only one-fourth number needed graduate each year.

OEK Brief No. 206
WORK Brief No. 208

ENGINEERS, MINING

May aid in search for mineral deposits. Determine whether deposit exists and is rich enough to mine; determine position of mine, methods of transportation to surface and extraction. In charge of safety, equipment, personnel, mining operations.

Wherever mineral resources are mined, especially in Pennsylvania, Texas, California, New York, West Virginia, Ohio, Louisiana, Minnesota. May also work for government agencies, in colleges or universities. May be private consultants.

About 5000, almost all men.

College degree in mining engineering.

Energy, stamina, interest in and aptitude for math and science, reliability. May need state license.

College placement offices, professional journals and associations list openings. Direct application to mining concerns. Summer job may lead to full-time work.

Good. May start as section head, foreman, or manager; move to supervisor, manager, administrator, examining engineer, consultant, research specialist.

Starting average: $10,000.

A slow increase expected as lower-grade ores are mined and industry devises uses for minerals that currently have few or none. Estimate 100 openings annually.

OEK Brief No. 207
WORK Brief No. 212

OCCUPATION	ENGINEERS, NUCLEAR	ENGINEERS, PETROLEUM
DUTIES	Perform engineering research and development with neutrons and radiation and with radioactive materials. May design nuclear equipment for testing, power plants, research projects. On site, interpret plans of physicists, scientists, designers for construction engineers and craftsmen; supervise loading of nuclear fuel into reactor.	Plan and supervise drilling for oil and natural gas. Help prepare drilling site, select method of drilling, direct workers in installing drilling rig and machinery, advise drilling personnel on technical matters, select method for getting oil and gas to surface, control rate of production.
WHERE EMPLOYED	Research centers owned by U.S. Atomic Energy Commission; companies that design and manufacture nuclear reactors.	Oil companies, manufacturers of oil-field equipment, universities, research laboratories. In oil-producing states; offshore operations in Gulf of Mexico; projects of U.S. companies in Middle East, Africa, South America, Canada.
NUMBER OF WORKERS	Undetermined.	About 16,000 men.
EDUCATION AND TRAINING	Some opportunities for those with bachelor's degree in mechanical engineering; master's in nuclear engineering preferred. AEC has information about numerous assistance programs for graduate work.	Bachelor's degree, preferably in petroleum engineering. Most companies conduct training programs for new engineers.
SPECIAL QUALIFICATIONS	Creativity, inquisitive mind, ability to analyze scientific problems, perseverance, mechanical aptitude, manual dexterity.	Mechanical aptitude, ingenuity, good judgment, resourcefulness, adaptability. Ability to supervise crew. Enjoy outdoor work.
WAYS TO ENTER FIELD	Some AEC contractors offer summer jobs to high school seniors, college students. Campus interviews; college placement office. Take federal civil service exam. Check with state employment service. AEC offers list of firms in atomic energy field; contact these employers direct.	University placement service, including campus interviews. Apply direct to petroleum companies. American Petroleum Institute can also provide job leads.
CHANCE OF ADVANCEMENT	Will depend on employer, type of projects. May become director of research facility, company executive.	Usually start as junior engineer and advance to senior engineer, to administrative posts in engineering, production, marketing, or other areas.
EARNINGS	Start: $10,000 a year. Experienced: $10,000–$15,000.	Start: $10,000; with master's degree, $12,000. Experienced: $13,000–$30,000.
SUPPLY AND DEMAND	Growing demand for nuclear engineers to meet research and development needs. AEC programs guarantee continuing expansion. Many corporations investigating use of atomic power in their industries.	Employment level expected to remain stable or increase slowly. Exploration and secondary recovery (obtaining additional oil from old fields) will offer most opportunity.
REFERENCES	OEK Brief No. 203 WORK Brief No. 218	OEK Brief No. 208 WORK Brief No. 236

ENGINEERS, SAFETY

Analyze, control, eliminate safety hazards to prevent personal injury and property damage in industrial plants, mines, commercial establishments, construction operations. Design and recommend means to prevent accidents, educate and train people in safety. May examine specifications for job procedures, machinery, equipment, structures from safety standpoint.

Industrial plants, mines; construction, distribution companies; casualty, fire insurance companies; government agencies throughout U.S., especially in highly industrialized areas.

20,000, almost all men.

High school diploma. College degree in engineering or safety engineering recommended. May substitute home study or special short-term courses. On-the-job training usually provided.

Maturity, good judgment, mental alertness, tact, persuasiveness.

Apply direct to mining, manufacturing, insurance, or other company, federal government agency, state labor department. Most government jobs require civil service exam.

Good opportunities to become head of safety department, chief engineer, plant manager.

Nonprofessionals: $9000–$10,000. Professionals: $15,000–$25,000.

Expect continued strong demand for these workers. There is a shortage of college-trained men who qualify as safety engineers.

OEK Brief No. 292
WORK Brief No. 285

ENGINEERS, SANITARY

Design, develop, administer systems and procedures to protect public health in such areas as sewage and refuse disposal, control of air and water pollution, food sanitation, insect and rodent control. May teach, do research.

Federal, state, and local government agencies; business and industrial concerns; engineering firms; colleges and universities.

Undetermined. About 185,000 civil engineers.

Civil engineering degree essential; graduate degree required for many positions.

Aptitude for science, math; mechanical aptitude; administrative ability; good judgment. May need state license.

Apply to civil service offices, local health or public works departments; direct to nongovernment employers. College placement service may help.

Good chance to advance to supervisory, administrative positions.

Start: $10,000–$11,000. Experienced: $13,000–$18,000. Top: $25,000 or more. Highest average salaries are in federal government.

Growing population will lead to increased demand for sanitary engineers. Present shortage likely to continue.

OEK Brief No. 250
WORK Brief No. 287

ENGINEERS, STATIONARY

Operate, maintain, and repair stationary engines, boilers, furnaces, generators, turbines, and other equipment. Inspect equipment regularly, check gauges and meters, make adjustments and repairs, keep records, supervise work.

Federal, state, and city government agencies; manufacturing and processing plants; public utilities; steamships; large buildings such as hospitals, office buildings, hotels, apartment houses, and schools.

About 200,000; less than 1% women.

High school preferred, plus 4-year apprenticeship or on-the-job training. Trade school helpful.

A few states and many cities require passing exam for state or local license. Mechanical ability, manual dexterity, accuracy, reliability, responsibility.

Job openings can be located through union and state employment offices, newspaper want ads, placement bureaus of trade schools, civil service offices.

Good for those who pass exam for higher class license and have special technical training. Can become supervisor, chief engineer, superintendent.

$2.84–$4.98 an hour.

No increase expected; replacement needs will create many openings. Best chances for those with technical training.

OEK Brief No. 177
WORK Brief No. 306

OCCUPATION	ENGINEERS, TRAFFIC	EXECUTIVE HOUSEKEEPERS
DUTIES	Plan, design, and develop traffic-control systems to prevent accidents, minimize congestion. Collect and analyze data, define problems, suggest solutions, implement, evaluate effectiveness of solutions. May teach, do research.	Supervise housekeeping staff. May hire and train new employees. Order supplies, take inventories, keep records, prepare budgets, report needed repairs, suggest improvements, draw up work schedules, inspect rooms. May be in charge of interior decoration.
WHERE EMPLOYED	State and local departments of highways and traffic; engineering firms; federal government agencies; colleges and universities; trade, business, and industrial organizations.	Hospitals, retirement homes, hotels and motels, school dormitories, department stores, industrial plants, medical and office buildings.
NUMBER OF WORKERS	Undetermined. About 185,000 civil engineers.	About 30,000 executive housekeepers and assistants in hotels alone. Mostly women, but number of men increasing.
EDUCATION AND TRAINING	College civil engineering degree essential; graduate work in traffic or highway engineering important.	High school education plus business experience or college work recommended. College degree becoming more important.
SPECIAL QUALIFICATIONS	Logical and analytical mind, aptitude for math, leadership and administrative abilities, tact, persuasiveness, flexibility, creativity, liking for detail work.	Ability to organize their own and others' activities, analyze and possibly improve procedures, make decisions, get along well with people, supervise others.
WAYS TO ENTER FIELD	College placement bureau helpful. Notices of openings appear in *Traffic Engineering*. Apply to civil service offices.	May start on housekeeping staff and work up. With adequate training, can start as executive assistant. Apply direct to hotel, hospital, or other employer.
CHANCE OF ADVANCEMENT	Good. Can become survey director, administrator, chief engineer, consultant.	Limited. May be transferred to a larger establishment; promoted to general service manager, director of plant operations.
EARNINGS	Start: $10,000–$11,000. Experienced: $13,000–$18,000. Top: $25,000 or more.	$4500–$10,000, varying with experience and size of establishment. May get free meals and laundry.
SUPPLY AND DEMAND	Present shortage of trained traffic engineers expected to continue. Little competition for competent men.	As number of hotels, luxury motels, and hospitals increases, more housekeepers are needed. Chances will be best for those with college training.
REFERENCES	OEK Brief No. 360 WORK Brief No. 326	OEK Brief No. 326 WORK Brief No. 115

FACTORY ASSEMBLERS

Following instructions or diagrams, attach component parts of manufactured items in correct place. Usually perform single operation. May weld, screw, solder, bolt, glue, cut, wire. Use hand and machine tools. May check own work.

Assembly plants throughout U.S. Practically every large manufacturing industry uses the assembly-line method of production.

About 865,000 assemblers; more than 40% women.

Grade school education is usually enough. On-the-job training may last a day to several weeks.

Ability to work rapidly and accurately, manual dexterity, patience, good eyesight, liking for routine.

State employment agencies, want ads in newspapers, direct application to personnel offices of factories.

Good chance to become skilled assembler, inspector, supervisor, foreman. With more training, can become technician.

$2.50–$3.75, depending on industry, area, experience. Slightly less for women.

In most industries, some increase in demand. High school graduates have best chance.

WORK Brief No. 117

FACTORY INSPECTORS

Check measurements, performance, quality of manufactured or processed items. Discover unsatisfactory materials, parts, or assembled pieces. May use measuring instruments, keep inspection records.

Almost every manufacturing and processing industry throughout U.S., especially in industrial areas.

About 665,000; 40% women.

High school graduates preferred. Good trade school, exceptional aptitude, production experience may compensate. On-the-job training.

Good natural or corrected eyesight, ability to pay attention to detail, accuracy, mechanical ability, tact.

State or private employment agencies, want ads, unions, or direct application to manufacturers. Many start as assemblers or production workers.

Those with ability, dependability, knowledge of newest testing techniques can become foremen or supervisors.

$2–$4.85 an hour, depending on skill and experience.

Demand will increase as production becomes more complex and standards more exacting. Machines will perform simpler inspection jobs.

OEK Brief No. 327
WORK Brief No. 118

FARM EQUIPMENT DEALERS

Assemble, display, demonstrate, sell, service, and repair farm equipment and machinery, such as tractors, combines, balers, cornpickers, irrigation equipment, portable farm buildings.

In rural areas in all parts of the country.

About 19,000.

High school graduation necessary. College or technical agricultural school training recommended. Farm equipment manufacturers also have training programs.

Good business sense, courtesy, tact, patience, reliability, honesty, familiarity with farm problems in area.

Apply directly to established dealer or manufacturer. Usually start as salesman.

Can expand business, obtain additional dealerships.

Vary with prosperity of area and ability of dealer. About $20,000–$25,000 average.

Demand for men who understand agriculture, business, and management.

OEK Brief No. 232
WORK Brief No. 119

OCCUPATION	FARMERS	FARMERS, VEGETABLE
DUTIES	Raise crops, animals, poultry; produce dairy products. Select equipment, seed, fertilizer, or feed to be used. Plant, cultivate, harvest crops; feed and care for livestock; maintain equipment. Plan development. Market products.	Raise vegetables for wholesale marketing and processing. Prepare soil, plant seed or young plants, fertilize, cultivate, spray, irrigate, most of this by machine. Market crops. Repair buildings and equipment; buy supplies, equipment, services; keep records. May supervise hands who do the manual work.
WHERE EMPLOYED	Dairy, livestock, poultry, or specialized crop farms throughout U.S.	On farms throughout U.S. Greatest concentration in California, Florida, New Jersey, Michigan, Wisconsin. Farms are usually large, specializing in one or two vegetables.
NUMBER OF WORKERS	About 4 million farmers and farm managers.	Number difficult to determine. Some women.
EDUCATION AND TRAINING	High school graduation desirable. So is college, with major in agriculture.	High school education recommended; college training in horticulture advisable. Participation in 4-H and Future Farmers or summer farmwork provides good background.
SPECIAL QUALIFICATIONS	Good health, physical endurance, capacity for scientific knowledge and application. Ability to plan in long-range terms, saving money in prosperous years to absorb bad ones.	Mechanical ability, liking for outdoor work. Should have scientific knowledge of growing plants, be willing to experiment, be observant and informed on new developments, able to supervise field hands, have some business know-how.
WAYS TO ENTER FIELD	Lacking family farm to work on, one may become a hired hand; or start as tenant farmer, renting land and equipment; or work on shares, sharing profit with owner.	If one does not have family farm on which to start, get experience as a farm laborer; check with state employment service. Can start own business as tenant farmer or by leasing land; see want ads in local newspapers and farm publications; check farm organizations in preferred area.
CHANCE OF ADVANCEMENT	Acquire one's own farm. Make a success of own farm or join others in cooperative or corporate arrangement.	Become supervisor of laborers, farm manager. Buy small farm, gradually add to land holdings; buy into partnership or large company-owned operation.
EARNINGS	Vary, depending on size, location, product, conditions, and market. From a few hundred to $25,000 a year or more.	Earnings vary so much that meaningful estimates are difficult to make. A few farmers become wealthy; most achieve reasonable income; some barely exist.
SUPPLY AND DEMAND	Farmers decreasing in number as farms get bigger and mechanization increases. Related services and suppliers increasing.	Trend is toward larger and larger farms, reducing opportunities for beginners. Vegetable growers who want to operate on small areas near cities sometimes go into greenhouse production of crops.
REFERENCES	OEK Brief Nos. 43, 45, 48 WORK Brief Nos. 82, 252, 332	OEK Brief No. 48 WORK Brief No. 332

FBI AGENTS	FIRE FIGHTERS	FLIGHT ENGINEERS
Investigate violations of federal law, present information gathered to government lawyers; conduct security checks on potential federal employees; track internal enemies.	Extinguish fires, restricting property damage and loss of life. May specialize as truckmen, laddermen, hosemen, members of rescue teams, inspectors. Attend practice drills, maintain equipment, inspect buildings, educate public.	Monitor operation of more than 100 mechanical and electrical devices aboard airplane, perform before-takeoff inspections on almost 200 items, and in other ways assist pilot in providing hazard-free transportation. Make minor repairs in flight, keep flight log of engine performance, fuel consumption, other operations; make postflight inspection.
U.S. Department of Justice throughout U.S.	In cities or towns, usually over 10,000, that have a full-time fire department. Smaller communities often have one paid fire chief who commands volunteer firemen.	With almost 50 major airlines. Work in every state, but most are based in California, Florida, Illinois, New York, and Texas, where most long-distance flights of major lines originate and terminate.
About 8500.	More than 180,000 men are full-time fire fighters.	About 8000 men.
College degree required. Major in law or accounting. 14 weeks of on-the-job training.	High school graduation usually required. Several weeks training in firemen's school. Ongoing training in methods of fire prevention and control.	Two or more years of college preferred; course of ground and flight instruction approved by Federal Aviation Administration, or other training for certification. Airlines give several weeks training.
Age 23–40, U.S. citizen. Must pass oral, written, physical exams, character and loyalty check, have driver's license.	Physical stamina and agility, alertness, courage, mechanical aptitude. Ability to make quick and accurate judgments is necessary for officers.	Maturity, mental alertness, ability to think quickly and accurately under pressure, emotional stability, self-control, resourcefulness. Have commercial pilot's license, preferably with instrument rating; be certified by FAA; pass rigid physical exam.
Write to director of FBI in Washington for information about vacancies, time and place of exams, and how to apply.	Pass local civil service test including rigid physical exam, athletic performance, intelligence test. Military and volunteer fire-fighting experience helpful.	Those who feel they have all the qualifications can apply direct to airlines.
Can advance to greater responsibility as field supervisor, agent in charge of field office, inspector, administrative positions.	Promotion determined by performance and written tests. Lieutenant, captain, battalion chief, deputy or assistant chief, chief.	Almost automatic promotion to copilot after several years; in another 5–10 years to captain. With seniority they obtain the routes and schedules that pay most. A few become chief pilot or flight operations manager.
Start: $11,517. Top: about $24,000.	$6500–$9000. Officers earn more. Larger cities pay best.	Average: domestic flights, $1702 a month; international flights, $1920. Top: $3150 a month.
Low turnover. Many more applicants than jobs. Competition very tough, but those qualified are urged to apply.	Rapid increase due to growth of cities and villages, and trend to shorter on-duty hours. Competition heavy for openings.	Expect demand for these workers to grow slightly during 1970s. Thorough training is essential.
OEK Brief No. 55 WORK Brief No. 121	OEK Brief No. 52 WORK Brief No. 124	OEK Brief No. 305 WORK Brief No. 126

OCCUPATION	FLOOR COVERING INSTALLERS	FLORISTS
DUTIES	Install, replace, repair resilient tile, linoleum, and other sheet covering, and carpeting on floors. Inspect, clean, smooth floor surface. Cut, fit, install lining felt or padding. Place guidemarks; fit, match, paste down sheets or tiles. Tack down carpeting; may cut and sew. May install resilient wall and counter coverings. May specialize.	Buy, arrange, display, and sell flowers. Sometimes arrange flowers in churches, homes, and commercial establishments or demonstrate arrangements for clubs or classes. Some operate greenhouses.
WHERE EMPLOYED	Floor covering retailers, installation contractors, furniture and department stores that sell floor covering and installation service. Some are self-employed. Throughout U.S., especially in urban areas.	Throughout U.S., but primarily in cities.
NUMBER OF WORKERS	About 40,000 men. A few women are employed in carpet workrooms on sewing and related operations.	About 22,000 retail flower shops employ 100,000 people. About 50% are women.
EDUCATION AND TRAINING	High school education desirable. Can learn work through on-the-job training, short-term factory training school, trade school, home study course. 3- and 4-year apprenticeships in some cities.	High school graduation is advised. Additional training given on the job or in special schools. College is advised for shopowners.
SPECIAL QUALIFICATIONS	Agility, manual dexterity, average strength, some mechanical ability. Attention to detail, appreciation of good color and design. Preference for active, indoor work.	Artistic sense, manual dexterity, tact in dealing with the public. For a shopowner, good business sense and a thorough knowledge of flowers.
WAYS TO ENTER FIELD	Apply direct to floor-covering retailers, installation contractors, furniture and department stores. Watch newspaper ads; check with state employment service and union offices. May start as helper or laborer.	Secure a job with a florist through want ads, personal contact, or employment agency. Afterschool and summer work is good entry route.
CHANCE OF ADVANCEMENT	Opportunities to become crew foreman, installation manager, estimator, salesman. Some men establish own business as dealer or contractor.	Advancement in a shop is to assistant floral designer, designer, and manager. Opening one's own shop is a frequent goal.
EARNINGS	Union wage range: $6.50–$9 an hour (western U.S.). Apprentices usually start at half the journeyman rate.	Beginners: $85 a week. Skilled workers: $150 or more.
SUPPLY AND DEMAND	New buildings need floor coverings, old ones need periodic replacements. Shortage of these workers. Expect 2000 openings a year in 1970s.	Floral business continues to increase considerably each year. Great demand for part-time workers for holiday rush seasons.
REFERENCES	OEK Brief No. 14￼ WORK Brief No. 127	OEK Brief No. 233￼ WORK Brief No. 128

FOOD STORE WORKERS

Clean and stock shelves; check in food shipments and keep stockroom orderly; bag purchases and carry out to cars; build displays; work at checkout counter as cashier; bag, weigh, and price-mark fruits and vegetables. May take phone orders and gather items for delivery.

At grocery stores and supermarkets throughout the country.

More than 1.5 million.

High school diploma usually required for full-time work. Many stores give a few weeks of on-the-job training.

Outgoing personality; clerical ability, manual dexterity, physical stamina, courtesy, cheerfulness, neatness.

Apply to personnel offices of food chains or direct to independent food stores. Check with state employment agency and retail clerks union. For part-time jobs, stores often post notices in store window.

Very good. May advance to head clerk or checker, assistant department manager, department manager, store manager.

Vary according to location and size of store. Average: about $2.54 an hour. Range: baggers, $1.60; checkers, $3.60.

Growing demand and rapid turnover create many openings. Many part-time opportunities.

OEK Brief No. 332
WORK Brief No. 130

FOREMEN

Supervise and coordinate activities of blue-collar workers. Train new employees; maintain employee and production records, plan and schedule work loads, attend meetings, and prepare reports on production, cost, personnel, safety. See that safety rules are observed. May meet with union representatives. May work at same crafts as employees they supervise.

Most work in or near urban areas.

About 1½ million; 90% men.

No specific educational requirements. Most foremen rise through the ranks.

Ability to motivate employees, command respect, get along with people. Good judgment, ability to make decisions, reliability, sense of responsibility.

Either by starting as a laborer and working up or by earning a college degree and starting out in an industry as a foreman-in-training.

Promotion to a higher management position is usually the goal of a foreman. Experience, skill, and management will determine how fast and how far he can go.

Average from 10% to 40% above the highest-paid worker he supervises.

There will always be a place for foremen in industry. Expect at least 57,000 job openings a year throughout the 1970s.

OEK Brief No. 400
WORK Brief No. 132

FORESTERS

Forest development, management, and conservation. Frequently administrative. Safeguard forests, plan reforestation, estimate the amount of timber and its value, buy or sell timber, plan and supervise cutting. Teach, do research.

State and federal government agencies, pulp and paper mills, logging and lumber companies, sawmills, nurseries and tree-care services, universities. Especially in heavily wooded areas of the U.S.

About 26,000 in forestry and conservation; 2% women.

B.S. usually the minimum. Advanced degree necessary for research and teaching.

Outdoor interests, ability to deal with people and to endure vigorous physical activity. Must pass exam for government jobs.

Apply to civil service office or to companies. College placement bureau helpful. 1- or 2-year probationary period to determine suitability to the work.

Good. Can advance to district ranger, forest supervisor, managing forester; comparable position in research or forest work.

In industry: start, $5000–$10,000; top, $50,000. In government: foresters in charge of ranger district, $10,500–$19,600; in regional administration, $24,200–$35,600.

Growing demand, especially for people with advanced degrees. Expect at least 1000 openings a year. Competition increasing, however.

OEK Brief No. 50
WORK Brief No. 133

OCCUPATION	FORESTRY AIDES	FOUNDRY WORKERS
DUTIES	Assist foresters in managing and caring for public and private forest lands. Estimate amount, growth, value of timber by sampling techniques; mark timber for harvest; prune trees; spray trees to protect from insects and diseases; prevent and fight forest fires; conduct road surveys; maintain forest trails. May supervise timber sales, manage recreation facilities.	Make metal castings for use in other products. Work in one of five areas in foundry: molding, coremaking, melting, cleaning and finishing, and control. May be professional, technical, skilled, semiskilled, or unskilled worker.
WHERE EMPLOYED	About 40% in federal government, mainly Forest Service; 20% in state service; 40% in private industry—lumbering, logging, paper milling. Most work in Washington, California, Oregon, Idaho, Utah, Montana.	In independent foundries and foundry departments of other metalworking establishments.
NUMBER OF WORKERS	Estimated 13,000 men.	About 450,000.
EDUCATION AND TRAINING	High school diploma, plus 1- or 2-year specialized training program in technical institute, junior college, or ranger school; or work experience such as felling or planting trees, fighting forest fires.	A high school education or equivalent is usually necessary to qualify for 4- to 5-year apprenticeship. For some jobs informal on-the-job training is sufficient; diploma not required.
SPECIAL QUALIFICATIONS	Enthusiasm for outdoor work, physical stamina, ability to work without direct supervision. Some jobs require willingness to work in remote areas.	Good health, physical stamina, mechanical aptitude, manual dexterity, good eyesight, good judgment, accuracy.
WAYS TO ENTER FIELD	Check with U.S. and state civil service commissions about exams to qualify for these jobs. Apply to lumber, timber, paper companies. Forestry schools helpful in placement.	Apply to union or to joint apprenticeship committee. Want ads, state employment service, direct application to foundry are other ways to get started.
CHANCE OF ADVANCEMENT	Can advance to technician; also to supervisory or management positions, but these may require extensive experience or a bachelor's degree, or both.	Good. May upgrade skills, become foreman, shop supervisor.
EARNINGS	Beginners: $4500–$5000. Experienced: $8000–$8500.	Average: in iron and steel foundries, $3.73 an hour; in nonferrous foundries, $3.49.
SUPPLY AND DEMAND	Federal and state governments are expected to increase their numbers of aides into the mid-1970s. Industry will also need more of these workers as their businesses expand.	No significant increase expected, but thousands of replacement jobs will be available.
REFERENCES	OEK Brief No. 340 WORK Brief No. 134	OEK Brief No. 103 WORK Brief No. 135

FUNERAL DIRECTORS	GARDENERS AND GROUNDS KEEPERS	GEOGRAPHERS
Take care of details of funerals: assist family, arrange service, help select casket, get death certificate, arrange and supervise burial. May embalm and dress body. Manage funeral home: keep accounts, purchase supplies, advertise. May teach mortuary science.	Plant and care for gardens, lawns, shrubbery, trees. May plan layout, follow landscape architect's blueprints or established patterns; care for greenhouse or conservatory; select seeds, bulbs, seedlings, cuttings; prepare soil, plant, water; apply fertilizer, insecticide, weed killer; cut, trim, prune lawn, plants, shrubs, trees. May make minor tool repairs.	Study physical, economic, political, social, cultural characteristics of regions of the earth and their inhabitants. Collect data for, plan, and construct maps. Many teach, do research. May specialize in one area of geography.
Funeral homes, mortuary schools, and companies that manufacture or distribute mortuary supplies and equipment.	Country estates, cemeteries, arboretums, parks, greenhouses, outdoor recreational facilities; industrial plants, shopping centers, housing developments, retirement communities, resort hotels; landscaping, gardening businesses.	About ⅔ teach in colleges and universities. Government and industry employ the rest. Research may be done in foreign countries.
More than 65,000 licensed embalmers and funeral directors; 2% women.	1300 members in National Assn. of Gardeners, but thousands more are employed in this broad area. Most are men.	About 7000; 10% women.
State requirements vary, but most require high school plus 9–12 months mortuary school and at least 1-year apprenticeship.	No formal education requirements. Some vocational, trade school, or agricultural college training helpful for advancement. Parks and other employers usually give informal on-the-job training.	Bachelor's degree the minimum. Graduate degree required for many jobs.
Must pass exam for state license. Administrative ability, sincerity, tact, courtesy, emotional stability, well-groomed appearance, friendliness.	Love of plants and working in the soil, some native understanding of plant life, appreciation of natural beauty and of design and artistic effects, preference for active outdoor work.	Interest in natural and social sciences, inquiring mind, imagination, ability to make accurate judgments.
Placement services of mortuary schools, personal contacts, direct application to funeral homes, family partnership. Most start as embalmers.	State, federal, and many city jobs are filled through Civil Service Commission exams. Consult newspaper ads; check with state employment service; apply direct to employers known to have gardeners or whose property might indicate their need for one.	Through professional societies, college or teacher-placement bureaus, civil service offices. Can apply direct to private companies.
Can switch to better position, buy share in established business, open own funeral establishment.	To head gardener or foreman; to greenskeeper foreman or superintendent; to plantation foreman, maintenance foreman, landscaper, or apprentice horticulturist. Develop own business.	Good for those with advanced degrees. Can become professor, head of department, research project director, consultant.
Funeral directors average about $7000 a year, owners about $12,000.	Considerable variation by location and employer. Some start at $4000 a year. Experienced gardeners may earn $3.70 an hour; supervisors, $800 a month.	Start: $7600–$14,000, depending on education and employer. Teacher's salaries are lowest; Ph.D.s in government highest. Can augment salary with royalties, consultant fees.
Demand for graduates somewhat greater than supply. About 1500 openings a year expected.	Reliable, experienced gardeners are always in demand, but no great increase in employment is foreseen.	Greatest opportunities in teaching, but openings increasing in all fields. Competition light.
OEK Brief No. 132 WORK Brief No. 137	OEK Brief No. 330 WORK Brief No. 140	OEK Brief No. 185 WORK Brief No. 142

OCCUPATION	GEOLOGISTS	GEOPHYSICISTS
DUTIES	Identify fossils. Study history, composition of rocks; physical, chemical properties of mineral deposits; form of earth's surface and events that changed it. Locate, develop mineral resources, sites for bridge foundations, tunnels, wells.	Study the earth's physical characteristics, such as its electric, magnetic, and gravitational fields; the earth's interior heat flow and vibrations; and solar radiation. Use complex precision measuring instruments and electronic computers to record and process data. May search for oil and mineral deposits, track satellites, probe oceans.
WHERE EMPLOYED	About 60% work for the petroleum and natural gas industries, the rest for other industries, federal and state agencies, universities, colleges, and museums. Some self-employed as consultants.	For petroleum and natural gas industries; federal and state agencies, colleges and universities. A few are self-employed as consultants.
NUMBER OF WORKERS	About 29,000, almost all men.	About 8000.
EDUCATION AND TRAINING	Bachelor's degree minimum. Advanced degree required for specialization. Ph.D. almost essential for research, professorships.	Bachelor's degree with major in geophysics or one of its specialties a must for beginning jobs in exploration geophysics. Ph.D. usually required for teaching and research positions.
SPECIAL QUALIFICATIONS	Interest and aptitude in science, inquiring mind, ability to visualize in three dimensions. Good health, physical stamina, liking for outdoor work.	Interest and aptitude in science; energy, physical stamina, liking for outdoor work, willingness to travel.
WAYS TO ENTER FIELD	Direct application to companies, school placement offices, federal and state civil service offices. Watch ads in professional journals. Summer jobs provide a good start.	Direct application to companies, school placement offices, federal and state civil service offices. Ads in professional journals. Summer jobs provide good start.
CHANCE OF ADVANCEMENT	Good with advanced degree, ability. From field or laboratory assistant to research worker, administrator, executive, consultant.	Good with advanced degree and ability. May be promoted to chief of exploration party, administrator, consultant, full professor, depending on employer.
EARNINGS	Start: with a B.S., about $720 a month; master's, $885. Ph.D.s earn considerably more. Median: $15,000.	Start: with bachelor's degree, $7500–$9000; with master's, $9000–$10,500; with Ph.D., $11,000–$13,000.
SUPPLY AND DEMAND	Most demand for geologists with advanced degrees. Employment prospects look good, with about 600 job openings each year.	A growing field. Expect at least 500 job openings a year through the 1970s.
REFERENCES	OEK Brief No. 184 WORK Brief No. 143	OEK Brief No. 331 WORK Brief No. 144

GLAZIERS	GUARDS AND WATCHMEN	GUIDANCE COUNSELORS
Cut glass and mirrors to correct size; smooth, polish, and install in buildings, homes, furniture, automobiles, and boats.	Patrol grounds and buildings, check doors and windows, observe loading of merchandise to prevent theft. Protect displays, give information, keep order. Accompany messengers who transport money and other valuables.	Help students and others make educational, vocational, personal plans and adjustments. Interview clients, give and interpret tests, conduct group guidance sessions. Collect and disseminate information on careers, schools.
Construction companies, glazing contractors, glass suppliers, and factories that make products using mirror, plate, or window glass.	Factories, office buildings, government and protective agencies, museums, banks. Throughout U.S., but more jobs available in cities and industrial areas.	Elementary and high schools, colleges and universities, government agencies, health and welfare agencies, counseling bureaus and agencies. Some are in private practice.
About 10,500 construction glaziers and 12,000 working in factories.	About 400,000 men. 70% work nights.	About 40,000 full-time school counselors; ⅓ women.
High school graduation recommended. 3-year apprenticeship, which includes 144 hours of classroom instruction a year.	High school education is sometimes required, but usually only the ability to read and write reports is necessary.	College degree in education or psychology plus, in many states, master's degree in guidance. May need teaching experience.
Manual dexterity; physical capacity to carry plates of glass and to climb, reach, stretch, and perform movements necessary for aligning and installing glass and mirrors.	Good powers of observation, reasonably good health, good hearing and eyesight, ability to make decisions and to move quickly in case of emergency, honesty, dependability, good judgment.	State teacher's and often counselor's certificate. Understanding of motivation and psychology, friendliness, warmth, emotional stability, empathy, tact, patience.
Apply direct to glazing contractors, to union, or to state employment service. Want ads may also list openings.	Apply to personnel departments. Watch want ads, visit state or private employment agencies, civil service commissions.	Many start as teachers. College placement services, notices in professional journals; direct application to school superintendents, agencies, civil service offices.
From apprentice to advanced apprentice to journeyman. Some chance to become foreman or contractor.	Limited. In federal government one can move up through three levels, each with more pay. In industry, to guard supervisor.	Good. Can become director of guidance for school or district; consultant; switch to better position in another school or agency.
Average: $6.08 an hour (construction glaziers). Apprentices start at half the journeyman rate.	Range: $1.99–$3.72 an hour.	Average: $12,051. College counselors earn more.
Expect rapid employment increase because of more building, modernization, and use of glass in architecture. Less work at construction sites, more in prefabricating.	The employment of guards will probably increase as industry continues to grow.	Demand increasing. Severe shortage of qualified counselors. Almost no competition for openings.
OEK Brief No. 363 WORK Brief No. 146	OEK Brief No. 297 WORK Brief No. 147	OEK Brief No. 244 WORK Brief No. 148

OCCUPATION	HISTORIANS	HOME ECONOMISTS
DUTIES	Study and analyze the records of the past. Teach, do research, write, and lecture. Identify, preserve, make available historical material of value. Prepare exhibits. Consult. Some specialize in a particular country or region, period of time, or other phase.	Give information and advice about home products and activities. May specialize in food, dietetics, clothing, child care, home appliances, household management. May teach, do research, plan menus, do public relations or welfare work.
WHERE EMPLOYED	Primarily in colleges and universities. Also in government agencies, nonprofit foundations, research councils, special libraries, historical societies, museums, large corporations, high schools.	Schools, colleges, universities, hospitals, hotels, restaurants, agricultural extension agencies, public utilities, food companies, home appliance manufacturers, mass media outlets, welfare agencies, testing laboratories.
NUMBER OF WORKERS	About 14,000, 85% of them in colleges and universities. Some women.	About 105,000. Most are women, but opportunities for men are increasing.
EDUCATION AND TRAINING	Ph.D. required for the more desirable positions in teaching, research, museums, libraries.	College degree in home economics necessary. Graduate degree usually required for research directors, nutritionists, college teachers.
SPECIAL QUALIFICATIONS	Above-average intelligence, ability to concentrate and relate facts. Inquiring mind, patience. persistence.	Scientific aptitude, interest in homemaking, initiative, efficiency. pleasing personality, patience, ability to work well with people. good grooming habits.
WAYS TO ENTER FIELD	Recommendation of college professor helpful for teaching positions. Civil service exams for government. College placement offices list openings.	College placement bureaus, civil service offices, newspaper want ads, direct application to employers.
CHANCE OF ADVANCEMENT	From instructor to assistant professor, associate professor, professor. Can become research director, administrator.	Excellent. One field where women can easily advance to top positions.
EARNINGS	From $13,000 (median) for instructors to $25,000 for full professors. Government work: $12,000–$20,000, according to degree and experience.	Secondary schools: $6800–$8600. Colleges and universities, business: $7000–$15,000. Government: $7000–$15,000.
SUPPLY AND DEMAND	Good opportunities for those with Ph.D. Considerable competition among those with master's. Demand for college teachers rising.	Not enough graduates to fill available jobs. Greatest demand in secondary education. Not too competitive; high turnover. Over 8000 openings a year.
REFERENCES	OEK Brief No. 377 WORK Brief No. 151	OEK Brief No. 6 WORK Brief No. 153

HORTICULTURISTS

Develop new and improved varieties of fruits, nuts, vegetables, flowers, shrubs, ornamental plants, other nursery stock. Try to find better methods of breeding, growing, harvesting, storing, transporting horticultural crops. Usually specialize in particular plant or particular technical problem such as plant breeding.

Colleges, universities, state and federal governments, nurseries, seed growers, conservatories, parks.

Probably over 7000, mostly men.

Bachelor's degree in horticulture adequate for beginning jobs. Advancement requires more education, preferably Ph.D. degree, especially for college teaching and independent research.

Interest in and curiosity about living things, especially plant life; keen observation; logical thought processes; infinite patience. Be able to communicate findings simply and clearly in writing and speaking.

Campus interviews, college placement service, recommendation of professors; direct application to seed companies or other private employers; civil service applications.

Experienced scientists may become professors, researchers, administrators in various capacities. Some become consultants, authors, owners of businesses.

Beginners can earn $7000 or more a year; beginners with a Ph.D., $8500–$10,000. May supplement salary by writing, speaking, consulting, special research.

Strong demand for men and women with advanced degrees. New graduates with bachelor's degree will find many opportunities to work as research assistants or technicians during graduate study.

OEK Brief No. 376
WORK Brief No. 154

HOSPITAL ADMINISTRATORS

Direct and coordinate all activities of hospital; responsible for budget and accounting, personnel, public relations, purchasing. Coordinate professional, technical, clerical, service, and maintenance staffs.

In hospitals throughout U.S., 1/3 of them government. A few teach in universities. Others work for health insurance companies, hospital and health associations.

About 17,000 administrators and assistants; 20% women.

Most hospitals require master's degree in hospital administration. This includes 1-year residency.

Tact, patience, administrative ability, leadership, integrity, good judgment. emotional maturity, responsibility, physical stamina, drive.

College placement service, medical placement agencies; help of professor, experienced administrator. Openings sometimes listed in hospital journals.

Start as department head or assistant administrator. Advancement limited after becoming administrator. Can switch to larger hospital.

Start: $10,000–$13,000. Experienced administrators: $10,000–$30,000.

Demand increasing as more hospitals are built. Much competition for top jobs.

OEK Brief No. 235
WORK Brief No. 155

HOSPITAL ATTENDANTS (AIDES AND ORDERLIES)

Make beds, carry trays, take pulse rates and temperatures, give baths and alcohol rubs, answer call lights of patients, supply and empty washbasins and bedpans, feed helpless patients, do other duties assigned by supervisor.

Hospitals, nursing homes, sanitariums.

About 830,000; 75% women.

High school education preferred. On-the-job training lasts several days to 3 months.

At least 17, in good health. A liking for people, stability, maturity, patience, tact, understanding.

Apply to hospitals and nursing homes. Civil service offices, state employment agencies, want ads will list available jobs.

Without additional training, very small. Valuable experience for nursing or other health jobs, however.

Average $74–$80.50 a week, depending on area and hospital. Men generally earn more than women.

The demand is great as health services increase. Expect over 111,000 job openings a year.

OEK Brief No. 236
WORK Brief No. 156

OCCUPATION	HOTEL AND MOTEL WORKERS	HOUSEHOLD WORKERS
DUTIES	Work in one of several departments: *housekeeping*, as maid, porter, houseman, linen-room attendant, laundry-room worker; *front office staff*, as room clerk, key clerk, mail clerk, information clerk; *lobby staff*, as bellman, doorman, elevator operator.	Housekeepers or butlers manage entire household; maids clean, make beds, do laundry, prepare and serve food; nursemaids concerned mainly with child care; caretakers and housemen keep yard and house clean and in good repair; personal maids or valets perform services such as caring for employer's clothing, keeping personal quarters tidy.
WHERE EMPLOYED	In hotels and motels throughout the U.S.	In private homes and with household cleaning-service firms. Some work full time for one employer; day workers, by day or hour. About 10% live in employer's home. ¾ of all workers employed in urban areas; ½ of total in South; smallest number in West.
NUMBER OF WORKERS	More than 870,000.	1½ million, about 4% men.
EDUCATION AND TRAINING	No specific educational requirements, but high school diploma will be an aid to promotion. On-the-job training.	No formal education requirements. Home economics courses in high schools, vocational schools, junior colleges, and training sponsored by welfare agencies and state employment services are all helpful.
SPECIAL QUALIFICATIONS	Patience, tact, courtesy, friendliness, neat appearance, honesty.	For women, ability to cook, sew, wash, iron, clean house, care for children. For men, manual dexterity, mechanical skill. For both, ability to operate electrical and mechanical household equipment, neatness, ability to organize work, honesty.
WAYS TO ENTER FIELD	Apply to personnel office of hotels or motels. May need references. Check want ads. Some part-time work available.	Get job leads from state employment service and private agencies that specialize in household employment. Check newspaper want ads.
CHANCE OF ADVANCEMENT	Good for men. With years of training and experience, can work up to manager.	Advancement other than by wage increases not available within households with only one or two domestics. May become supervisor or specialist for cleaning-service firms.
EARNINGS	Vary by location, size, and type of hotel or motel. About ½ of all workers covered by minimum wage law. Tips are a large part of earnings in some jobs.	Day workers: about $2 an hour; sometimes 1 meal and transportation costs in addition. Full-time and live-in workers: about $90 a week, plus maintenance.
SUPPLY AND DEMAND	Rapid increase expected. Most openings in high-turnover jobs—maids, porters, housemen.	Shortage, particularly of live-in workers. Rising demand for competent household workers expected for many years to come.
REFERENCES	OEK Brief No. 13 WORK Brief No. 158	OEK Brief No. 265 WORK Brief No. 160

INDUSTRIAL AND LABOR RELATIONS WORKERS

Industrial relations workers formulate personnel policy, recruit and train employees, keep records, administer wages and benefits for a company or agency. Labor relations workers represent government, labor, or management in collective bargaining and contract administration, interpret union contracts, see that labor laws are observed, settle grievances.

Private companies, labor unions, government agencies, colleges and universities throughout U.S., especially in industrial areas.

More than 70,000 in private industry, 29,000 federal employees; some in college teaching, some with labor unions.

Bachelor's degree in industrial relations, personnel, or business administration. Graduate or law degree usually required for top positions.

Capacity for independent thinking, ability to analyze what makes a worker enthusiastic and able to do his job well, tact, sincerity, responsibility.

Start as employment interviewer, job analyst, personnel assistant, or trainee in any of these fields. Summer jobs in production provide good experience. Representatives of organized labor may be union officials or business agents.

Excellent for capable young men. At least 7–10 years experience necessary to become industrial relations director.

$8000–$50,000, depending on employer and experience. Government jobs usually pay slightly less.

Competition is keen, especially without graduate work in a related field. The need is great, however, and will continue to increase.

OEK Brief No. 255
WORK Brief No. 165

INDUSTRIAL HYGIENISTS

Research on industrial hygiene problems, development of methods to eliminate danger due to radiation, poisons, fumes, or dust in the air and to prevent strain from noise or other environmental conditions.

Public health agencies, labor unions, industries, insurance companies, consulting firms, colleges and universities.

About 2200; very few women.

B.S. the minimum requirement, with major in biological or physical science. Graduate work required for top jobs.

Interest in science, ability to analyze situations quickly, patience, tact, pleasant manner, ability to be firmly convincing.

College placement offices and the American Industrial Hygiene Association have lists of available jobs. Application could also be made to city and state governments.

Excellent. Experience, ability, and graduate study required for top positions.

Starting average: $14,000. Experienced average: $22,000.

There are not enough trained people to fill the demand in this field.

OEK Brief No. 217
WORK Brief No. 163

INSTRUMENT MAKERS (MODELMAKERS)

Make experimental and custom-built mechanical instruments. Work from blueprints, sketches, verbal instructions, ideas of scientists, engineers. Make parts, assemble, test, Use hand and machine tools, precision measuring instruments.

Instrument manufacturers, federal government, university and commercial research laboratories. Primarily in large cities, particularly New York, Boston, Los Angeles, Chicago, Washington, Philadelphia.

Estimated 8000. Some women; more could qualify if they had high school shop courses.

High school education preferred, with math, science, machine shop. 4- or 5-year apprenticeship or on-the-job training.

Strong interest in mechanics and above-average manual dexterity. Initiative, resourcefulness, conscientiousness, spatial imagination, reasoning ability.

Apply direct to employers. State and private employment agencies and Civil Service Commission list openings. May start as machinist, machine-tool operator.

About 10 years experience to attain top skill. With additional training, can become technician, supervisor.

$3.50–$5.30 an hour for skilled instrument makers. Apprentices receive about half this amount.

Small field, but considerable expansion expected as instruments become even more necessary for research, industry, armed forces. Expect 400 openings a year.

OEK Brief No. 27
WORK Brief No. 167

OCCUPATION	INSURANCE ADJUSTERS	INSURANCE AGENTS
DUTIES	Make sure policy covers claim; arrange for any necessary emergency measures; secure written evidence of loss; examine every detail regarding cause and extent of loss; determine, with the insured, the amount owed to him.	Find prospects, interview them, discover policy best suited to their needs and ability to pay, sell the policy. Arrange for loans on policies. May file claims, help arrange finances in emergencies, collect premiums.
WHERE EMPLOYED	Insurance companies, adjustment bureaus, independent adjustment organizations throughout U.S., particularly in heavily populated areas.	Throughout U.S., especially where population is expanding and in industrial centers. Life agents usually represent only one company. Those selling casualty and property insurance may represent many.
NUMBER OF WORKERS	About 114,000.	Approximately 350,000 agents and brokers; 10% women.
EDUCATION AND TRAINING	High school is required; sometimes college or even law training. In-service training programs are also given.	Most agents hired in recent years have had some college training. Beginning agents usually receive training courses.
SPECIAL QUALIFICATIONS	Tact, sympathy, courtesy, patience, knowledge of human nature, ability to inspire confidence, sound judgment, keen observation, resourcefulness, alertness.	Sales ability, friendliness, tact, sincerity, self-confidence. Ability to plan one's own time and be self-motivating. Meet requirements for state license.
WAYS TO ENTER FIELD	Minor adjusting jobs open to college graduates. Without college or experience, begin as a clerk. After 2 or 3 years experience, may qualify as trainee in claims work.	Apply to insurance companies or to local agencies. Possibly begin by selling part time until you have enough contacts to support yourself full time.
CHANCE OF ADVANCEMENT	With ability, can advance through branch office to home office, to manager of claims department; start own adjustment service.	Excellent for the ambitious. Competition for sales is keen. May become assistant manager or manager of an agency office; regional supervisor overseeing agencies in a specific geographical area. A few become company executives.
EARNINGS	Range: $7300–$11,800. Average: $9100. Supervisors: $9200–$14,600.	Guaranteed income during training; thereafter, commissions only. Experienced: $8000–$20,000. Top: $30,000 or more.
SUPPLY AND DEMAND	As the insurance industry continues to grow, so will the opportunities for good adjusters.	Expect 16,000 job openings a year through the 1970s.
REFERENCES	OEK Brief No. 238 WORK Brief No. 170	OEK Brief No. 118 WORK Brief No. 171

INTERIOR DESIGNERS AND DECORATORS

Plan decor and functional arrangement of interiors; coordinate selection of furniture, draperies, floor coverings, interior accessories of residential and commercial structures, ships, aircraft. May submit sketches of plans, estimate costs, purchase materials, oversee work. Designers plan complete layout of rooms within wallspace allowed; may re-design entire interior.

Department stores, hotel and restaurant chains, architects, furniture and textile manufacturers and stores, antique dealers, office-supply houses. Many decorators have own studios or shops.

About 15,000; 50% are women.

2- or 3-year course in art school or design institute, or B.A. in fine art. Some employers require 1–3 years on-the-job training.

Artistic sense, imagination. Knowledge of furniture, fabrics, rugs, and accessories. Salesmanship, ability to work with people, patience. Normal color vision.

Apply to decorating firms, department or furniture stores. Will probably start as receptionist, draftsman, comparison shopper, workroom helper, salesperson.

Slow. Can become department head or supervisor, open own decorating establishment. Depends on talent, sales ability.

Start: $5200. Some experience, talent: $15,000 or more. Top: $25,000 or more.

The demand should increase for well-trained and qualified people. About 700 openings a year.

OEK Brief No. 8
WORK Brief No. 173

JEWELERS

Make, repair, buy, and sell jewelry. May work exclusively in repair shops. In factories, make the models and tools necessary for large-scale production.

Shops that sell and repair jewelry throughout the country. Primarily in or near large cities. Manufacture of fine jewelry centered in New York City. Costume jewelry made in many metropolitan areas.

Estimated 15,000 skilled workers in hand manufacture and repair; a few women.

Trade school courses, 3- or 4-year apprenticeship, or on-the-job training.

Patience, good eyesight, eye-hand coordination, manual dexterity, mechanical ability, honesty, and a liking for detail work.

Become an apprentice. The firm to which you are apprenticed will probably keep you on as a jeweler. School placement bureau may be helpful.

Can become all-round jeweler, able to make or repair any kind of jewelry. In factories, model or tool maker, foreman. Open own shop.

Repairmen in retail stores, trade shops: $80–$240 a week. Manufacturing jewelers: inexperienced, $2 an hour; journeymen, $3.35–$4.55.

Skilled jewelers have little trouble finding jobs. Newcomers might have some difficulty, as the field is not fast-growing. Only about 500 openings a year.

OEK Brief No. 200
WORK Brief No. 174

KITCHEN HELPERS

Assist cooks, chefs, bakers. May measure, mix, wash, chop vegetables and salad ingredients; wash dishes by hand or operate dishwashing machine; do a variety of other tasks under supervision.

In nearly every business establishment that serves food.

Undetermined. About 2.5 million in restaurant jobs.

No specific educational requirements. On-the-job training.

Good health, physical stamina.

Want ads, direct application.

Good. With initiative and ability can advance to cook's helper, cook or chef, baker, waiter, bartender.

$1.53–$3.20 an hour.

Rapid increase expected. High turnover, thousands of jobs available.

WORK Brief No. 176

OCCUPATION	LABORERS, CONSTRUCTION	LATHERS
DUTIES	Perform manual labor in construction work; load, unload, move tools or materials, shovel and move earth, dismantle scaffoldings, pour concrete, clean tools and work areas, perform other simple tasks under direction of a skilled craftsman, foreman, or building superintendent.	Install base for plaster on ceilings and walls. Build framework, fasten to building, attach laths to framework. Cut openings for electrical outlets, heating ducts, plumbing. Install metal reinforcements in corners to guide plasterers.
WHERE EMPLOYED	General and special-trade contractors in the construction industry, public utilities, state and municipal public works and highway departments throughout U.S.	With lathing and plastering contractors and general contractors throughout U.S. Some work outside construction, as in making lath backings for plaster display materials or scenery.
NUMBER OF WORKERS	About 815,000 men.	About 30,000, mostly men.
EDUCATION AND TRAINING	No minimum educational requirements. High school graduates have best chance of advancing. On-the-job training.	High school desirable. 2-year apprenticeship recommended.
SPECIAL QUALIFICATIONS	Physical strength and agility, good health, stamina, liking for outdoor work.	Manual dexterity and eye-hand coordination. Physical stamina and ability to reach, climb, be on feet all day, withstand cold and drafts in unfinished buildings.
WAYS TO ENTER FIELD	Apply to contractor or skilled tradesman for job as laborer or helper. Want ads, state employment service sometimes list job openings.	Apply for work direct to lathing contractors. Union offices, labor-management apprenticeship committees, state employment agencies list openings.
CHANCE OF ADVANCEMENT	Some chance to become journeyman. Some laborers become helpers, and a few can in time acquire skilled status.	To crew foreman, lathing superintendent. Start own contracting business.
EARNINGS	$2.10–$5.45 an hour, depending on location. Unlike apprentices' wages, laborers' wages do not automatically go up with experience.	$4.90–$7.23, depending on location. Apprentices usually start at half the journeyman rate.
SUPPLY AND DEMAND	Number of laborers expected to increase slowly. Need about 26,000 men a year.	Employment expected to increase rapidly despite use of prefabricated materials. Competition for apprenticeships strong.
REFERENCES	OEK Brief No. 109 WORK Brief No. 73	OEK Brief No. 337 WORK Brief No. 178

LAUNDRY WORKERS

Weigh bundles; mark each item for identification; sort by colors and fabrics; operate washing machines, extractors that remove water, drying machines; shake flatwork; feed ironers; fold; finish by hand or machine; mend; assemble for customers; wrap bundles.

With 45,000 commercial, industrial, institutional, coin-operated, and other laundries throughout U.S. ⅓ of all laundry workers are employed in cities of 500,000 or more.

Approximately 630,000 laundry and dry-cleaning operatives. About 66% of laundry workers are women.

Eighth-grade education usually adequate. Supervisory or office jobs may require a high school diploma. A few days training usually given.

Good coordination, manual dexterity, speed, physical strength, and endurance.

Apply to laundries. Want ads sometimes list openings. State employment service may be helpful.

With experience, work up through jobs that pay more. Additional training usually necessary to become supervisor or plant manager.

Average: $2.16 an hour. Plant managers: to $13,000 a year.

Moderate growth expected. Supervisory workers will have best opportunities.

OEK Brief No. 175
WORK Brief No. 179

LAWYERS

Give legal counsel and advice to individuals, corporations, officials; represent them in court; negotiate settlements out of court; draw up legal documents; act as guardians, trustees, executors. May specialize in one branch of law.

About 75% are in private practice or partnership. The rest are salaried, working in government, insurance, banking, real estate, industry, unions, or teaching in law schools.

About 286,000; 3% women.

Varies from the minimum of 5 years (2 of prelaw plus 3 of law school) to more desirable 7 years (4 years college plus 3 of law school).

Must pass bar exam to get state license. Logical, self-confident, persuasive, able to get along with people. Speaking and writing ability helpful.

Begin as associate or assistant in established law office. Possibly work for local or federal government. Apply direct to prospective employers or to civil service office.

May become partner or open own office. May specialize, represent single client or client group; become judge or other public official.

In salaried employment: start $6000–$10,000; with experience, $8500–$25,000. Attorneys in industry and law firms tend to earn more than those in private practice.

Many more graduates than openings every year. Competition keen. Many enter business or teach. Still room for those with ability.

OEK Brief No. 9
WORK Brief No. 180

LIBRARIANS, MEDICAL RECORD

Plan, prepare, maintain, analyze, coordinate records and reports on patients' illnesses and treatments. May develop auxiliary records, compile statistics, assist in research, manage department.

Private and government hospitals, large clinics, medical research centers, health departments, and insurance companies. Mostly in or near large cities.

Over 13,000. Almost all are women, but number of men growing.

2–4 years of college, or nursing degree, plus approved 1-year course in medical record library science. B.S. also offered.

Good judgment, integrity, ability to work efficiently under pressure, mental agility, liking for detail. Registered upon passing professional association exam.

Apply to hospitals, employment agencies that specialize in medical personnel, or nearest civil service office. Want ads in medical journals, newspapers.

More and more hospitals are adding medical record librarians to their regular staff. Can advance to supervisory or administrative positions.

Start: about $8000 a year. Experienced: to $15,000.

Not enough workers to meet present demand. Excellent chances. High school graduates can start as assistants to librarians.

OEK Brief No. 145
WORK Brief No. 204

OCCUPATION	LIBRARIANS, PUBLIC	LIBRARIANS, SPECIAL
DUTIES	Select books, pamphlets, periodicals, other items to be loaned to patrons; organize material in the most readily accessible manner; keep records of loans; assist those seeking information; do reference or research work.	Gather pertinent information on or related to a particular subject, organize it for ready reference, help people use it to advantage. Do research and reference work. May prepare bibliographies, translations, abstracts.
WHERE EMPLOYED	In 8000 public libraries and branches throughout U.S.	Government agencies, industrial companies, professional and trade associations, communications media, and the like.
NUMBER OF WORKERS	About 26,000; 85% women.	About 17,700; 75% women.
EDUCATION AND TRAINING	At least 4 years college. Master's degree in library science preferred; usually required for best posts.	At least 5 years college: bachelor's degree plus one year of study for master's in library science.
SPECIAL QUALIFICATIONS	Interest in books and people, intellectual curiosity, resourcefulness, accuracy, patience, courtesy. May have to pass civil service exam.	Above-average intelligence, patience, interest in subject. Ability to analyze facts, organize information.
WAYS TO ENTER FIELD	Placement service of library school. List of openings published in library association journals. Civil service office of local government.	Placement services of library schools or Special Libraries Association, whose periodical, Special Libraries, lists openings.
CHANCE OF ADVANCEMENT	Good. To supervisor, department head, branch librarian, director of county or city library.	To chief librarian in large library. Can switch to another organization to start or expand library.
EARNINGS	Starting average: $10,000. Experienced: to $30,000.	Starting average: $10,000. Experienced: to $30,000.
SUPPLY AND DEMAND	Many more openings than librarians to fill them. Good opportunities expected to continue.	About 20 job openings for every library school graduate. For special librarians, competition is practically nil.
REFERENCES	OEK Brief No. 10 WORK Brief No. 183	OEK Brief No. 189 WORK Brief No. 183

LIBRARIANS, TAPE

Classify, catalog, file, and charge out thousands of reels of magnetic tape used to store information in electronic data-processing installations. May devise storage system. Keep records, check tapes for damage, purge tapes to be discarded.

Manufacturing companies, financial organizations, public utilities, department stores, data-processing service centers. In and near cities and towns.

Small but growing number of workers.

High school diploma the minimum; some college preferred. Courses in data processing helpful. On-the-job training.

Clerical ability, accuracy, liking for detail, ability to work systematically, tolerance of routine.

See newspaper ads, state employment service. Apply direct to organization having data-processing installation. May start as coding clerk, file clerk, messenger, machine operator.

Limited. Some chance to become computer operator, supervisor, programmer.

Range: about $100–$140 a week.

Growing demand for tape librarians as more data-processing systems are installed. Considerable competition for positions.

OEK Brief No. 358
WORK Brief No. 183

LIBRARY TECHNICIANS

Give library patrons information on library services, facilities, and rules. Help locate books, answer some types of reference questions. May help catalog and order books, arrange displays, operate audiovisual and data-processing equipment. May work at checkout desk; may supervise clerical staff.

In public, college, high school, elementary school, and special libraries throughout the country.

About 76,000.

A high school diploma necessary, some college preferred. May take 2-year program for associate of arts degree in library technology.

Interest in books and people, intellectual curiosity, resourcefulness, patience, courtesy. Typing skills extremely useful.

Direct application to libraries, college placement offices, ads in professional journals.

Limited. Responsibilities and salary may increase, but cannot move up to librarian without degree in library science.

Average: $5000–$7000 a year. Top: with training and experience, $10,000.

Field growing. Expect 7000 job openings a year throughout the 1970s.

WORK Brief No. 184

LIFE SCIENTISTS

Study structure, evolutionary development, behavior, and life processes of all living organisms. Emphasize the relation between plants, animals, and microorganisms and their environment. Specialize in agriculture, biology, or medicine. May teach, do research, consult, write, be involved in management or administrative work.

Colleges and universities, medical schools and hospitals, government departments, private industry. Most in Washington, D.C., and New York City.

About 180,000; 10% women.

A bachelor's degree necessary for beginning jobs; graduate degrees for advancement.

Scientific interest and aptitude, curiosity, perseverance, initiative, ability to express self orally and in writing.

College placement bureau, want ads in professional journals, personal contacts, state employment offices.

With doctor's degree, may advance to directorships in research and administration, full professorship in teaching.

Start: $6500–$14,000, depending on degree. Average for all: $15,000 a year. Salaries highest in private industry.

Rapid increase expected. Anticipate 10,000 job openings a year throughout the 1970s.

OEK Brief Nos. 180, 294
WORK Brief No. 186

OCCUPATION	LINEMEN	LITHOGRAPHERS
DUTIES	Install, maintain, repair telephone and power cables. Use power-driven hole-digging equipment, erect poles, climb poles to attach or repair cables. In some cities place cables in underground conduits. May inspect lines in rural areas.	Cameramen photograph material to be printed, artists retouch parts of the negative, strippers paste negatives together in proper arrangement for printing, platemakers expose film to sensitized plates, pressmen operate printing presses.
WHERE EMPLOYED	Telephone and telegraph companies, electric power companies throughout U.S.	Offset printing firms throughout U.S.
NUMBER OF WORKERS	44,000 telephone linemen and related workers; 80,000 electric utility linemen and related workers.	Estimated 80,000 journeyman lithographers.
EDUCATION AND TRAINING	High school or vocational school minimum requirement. Related classroom and on-the-job training provided.	4- or 5-year apprenticeship. High school graduation usually required. Technical or vocational school training helpful.
SPECIAL QUALIFICATIONS	Good health, agility, manual dexterity. Ability to distinguish colors, climb, stoop, work in all kinds of weather. May have to pass aptitude test and physical exam.	Normal or properly corrected vision, manual dexterity, some mechanical aptitude.
WAYS TO ENTER FIELD	Apply to telephone or power company. Want ads, state employment service may be helpful.	Printers, union offices, want ads, state and private employment offices, direct application. High school counselor may help.
CHANCE OF ADVANCEMENT	Excellent for those who keep up with changes in the industry. Can transfer to telephone installer, repairman; advance to foreman.	May become shop foreman, general superintendent, estimator, production manager.
EARNINGS	Telephone linemen: $2.71–$3.33 an hour. Light and power industries: average $5.05.	Vary with specific occupation and locality. Range: $2.96–$8.20 an hour.
SUPPLY AND DEMAND	Slight increase expected in workers needed in electric power industry; decrease in telephone industry. Much competition for openings, as job appeals to many.	Moderate increase expected in demand for lithographers. Need at least 2600 new workers each year.
REFERENCES	OEK Brief No. 28 WORK Brief No. 187	OEK Brief No. 287 WORK Brief No. 225

MACHINE PARTS PROGRAMMERS

Prepare coded paper tapes for numerically directed automatic machine tools. Inspect parts to see that they conform to specifications.

In all machine shops using numerically controlled machine tools.

Undetermined; a very small number of the 1.2 million workers in machining occupations.

A high school or trade school education plus extensive machine shop experience.

Mechanical aptitude, manual dexterity, mathematical ability, accuracy.

Start as an apprentice; work up to parts programmer after several years experience and special training.

May advance to head of programming team.

Equal to or higher than machinist. Machinist range: $2.89–$4.86 an hour.

Excellent opportunities in this new field. Demand greater than supply of trained workers.

WORK Brief No. 193

MACHINE-TOOL OPERATORS

Use machine tools (such as lathes, milling machines, drill presses) to shape metal to exact dimensions. Set and operate machines, check dimensions of part being worked on. Usually specialize in one kind of machine and operation.

Most work in metalworking factories where machine parts are produced. Some work in job machine shops, and a few do maintenance work in machine shops of industrial plants. Mostly in industrial areas.

About 500,000 machine-tool operators; some women.

High school preferred but not essential. On-the-job training may last several weeks to 2 years.

Mechanical ability, accuracy, ability to read specifications and follow instructions, reliability, physical stamina.

Watch want ads. Apply to state employment office or to plants or shops employing machine-tool operators.

Limited. Can become layout man, foreman, or (with extra training) machinist, machine parts programmer, tool and die maker.

Class A operators, the most highly skilled, average $2.66–$3.61 an hour, depending on location and machine.

No employment growth expected, but about 9000 replacements needed annually.

WORK Brief No. 194

MACHINISTS

Shape metal parts to precise dimensions. Follow blueprints or specifications, select metal stock, lay out work. Use hand and machine tools to shape part, precision instruments to check work. May specialize in production or repair work.

Most are in production jobs in metalworking industries; some work in maintenance in various industries, some in machine shops that do jobs for factories. Mostly in industrial areas.

About 390,000 machinists and layout men. A few women.

High school preferred, plus 4-year apprenticeship. Some learn through informal on-the-job training.

Mechanical aptitude, manual dexterity, accuracy, dependability, ability to read blueprints and follow directions exactly.

Apply to union offices, directly to employers. Want ads, state employment service helpful. May start as machine-tool operator.

Can become tool and die maker, foreman, instrument maker. A few open their own job shops.

Journeymen usually average $2.89–$4.88 an hour, depending on geographical location.

Moderate increase expected. In addition, need about 16,000 replacements a year.

OEK Brief No. 30
WORK Brief No. 195

OCCUPATION	MAIL CARRIERS	MANAGERS, AIRPORT
DUTIES	Sort, deliver, and collect mail. May carry bag, push cart, drive truck or three-wheeled mailster. In rural areas, may sell stamps and money orders.	Plan and direct airport maintenance, operation, expansion, and improvement. See that safety and government regulations are observed. Supervise employees who work for airport. Supervise public relations, financial aspects of airport.
WHERE EMPLOYED	Throughout U.S. The majority work in large cities. A route may be a single office building or fifty miles of rural highway.	Large municipal airports; small private fields near rural communities; community and privately owned airports with limited number of scheduled flights.
NUMBER OF WORKERS	The U.S. Postal Service employs 546,000 full-time workers. About ⅓ of these are mail carriers.	About 500 full-time managers; 2500 part-time.
EDUCATION AND TRAINING	No definite requirements, but high school graduates preferred. Pre-Christmas rush season provides good trial period.	Vary with size of airport. High school necessary, college desirable. May take 1- or 2-year internship in airport management at airport.
SPECIAL QUALIFICATIONS	At least 18 and U.S. citizen. Good memory, health, physical stamina, ability to follow directions. Must pass physical and written exam.	Business and administrative ability; knowledge of field of flying and government regulations.
WAYS TO ENTER FIELD	Local civil service offices have information about the exam and other requirements. Beginners start as substitutes, advance to regulars as openings occur.	May start with a job in air traffic control, in airline communications or sales or, after internship, as assistant manager; or transfer from a supervisory position in a municipal system such as parks.
CHANCE OF ADVANCEMENT	Limited. Preferred routes go to those with seniority. Only 1% of city carriers are foremen or route examiners.	May move from small operation to larger; may expand existing operation.
EARNINGS	Regular city carriers: $3.90 an hour.	$8000–$25,000 or more, depending on size of airport. Median: $11,000–$12,000.
SUPPLY AND DEMAND	Volume of mail continually growing; foresee modest increase in employment. About 7900 openings a year.	Expanding airport facilities will create more managerial jobs—mostly for assistants or specialists in one part of the big operation.
REFERENCES	OEK Brief No. 263 WORK Brief No. 182	OEK Brief No. 271 WORK Brief No. 16

MANAGERS, APARTMENT BUILDING

Responsible for operating apartment building profitably. Direct and coordinate activities involving building maintenance, purchase of supplies, negotiation of leases, rent collection. Degree of involvement depends on size of building; may supervise many different types of workers.

Wherever there are apartment buildings.

About 70,000; ⅓ women.

A high school education necessary; college desirable for advancement. On-the-job training.

Keen business sense, leadership ability, responsibility, good judgment.

Check with local real estate boards.

With experience, can manage more than one building. With capital, start real estate management firm.

Vary with size, location, yearly income of building managed. Often live rent-free.

Good opportunities. Apartment buildings and condominiums are mushrooming, particularly in suburban areas.

WORK Brief No. 20

MANAGERS, HOTEL AND MOTEL

Responsible for operating hotel or motel profitably while making it as comfortable as possible for guests. Direct and coordinate all departments. May also have personnel, public relations, supervisory, and purchasing functions.

Hotels and motels throughout U.S.

About 200,000 managers and assistants.

College degree in hotel or business administration desirable. Many have less education but years of experience.

Administrative ability and business sense, responsibility, good judgment, ability to get along well with guests and employees.

Apply to hotel or personnel office of chain. College placement bureaus, state and private employment agencies helpful. May start as front-office clerk.

Can move to larger or better-paying hotel or motel; in chain, can obtain executive position.

Extremely wide range. Trainees: $8000–$12,000. Top: $50,000 or more.

Some increase in demand expected, especially in chain hotels and motels. College-trained young men will have advantage.

OEK Brief No. 313
WORK Brief No. 157

MANAGERS, INDUSTRIAL TRAFFIC

Manage and coordinate activities related to incoming and outgoing shipments. Select route, carrier; schedule and arrange for shipments; determine packaging, shipping methods; trace shipments, handle claims; direct record keeping.

Industrial companies (especially large manufacturers), government agencies, large department stores, mail-order companies. Some are self-employed as consultants.

About 18,000, mostly men.

High school sufficient for many positions; college degree preferred for jobs with big companies. In-service training.

Analytical mind, business ability, thoroughness, tact, initiative, good judgment; knowledge of transportation rates, regulations.

Apply direct to employer or to Civil Service Commission. May start as shipping or rate clerk, become supervisor, and finally manager.

Traffic manager is usually the top position in this field. Some can become vice-president in charge of transportation.

Trainees: to $8000. Experienced managers average $15,000–$30,000; in very large companies, $40,000. Salary determined partly by employer's transportation costs.

Moderate increase for alert, experienced men in this field. Jobs available at all levels.

OEK Brief No. 99
WORK Brief No. 327

OCCUPATION	MANAGERS, OFFICE	MANAGERS, RESTAURANT
DUTIES	Supervise clerical employees, plan and schedule office work, order equipment and supplies. Responsible for efficiency of work procedures, economy, personnel selection, morale, training; liaison with management.	Responsible for hiring, training, supervising, and maintaining efficiency of employees. Select supplies, food, equipment; keep accounts and records; plan or approve menu; enforce sanitation regulations; deal with customers.
WHERE EMPLOYED	Almost every kind of organization that employs a number of clerical workers has one or more office managers. In towns and cities throughout U.S.	Chain and independently owned restaurants, as well as hotels, department stores, clubs, and other establishments that serve food in quantity. Large cities and resort areas offer the most opportunities.
NUMBER OF WORKERS	More than 15,000 men and women.	More than 50,000 salaried restaurant managers, men and women.
EDUCATION AND TRAINING	College degree in business administration or accounting preferred, but those with high school diploma plus business school and experience may qualify.	College degree in restaurant or institutional management or business administration recommended. Some on-the-job training.
SPECIAL QUALIFICATIONS	Organizational and administrative abilities, analytical mind, even temper, tact, initiative, fairness, ability to get along well with and supervise people.	Initiative, imagination, ingenuity, salesmanship, head for business. Tact, good personality, ability to get along with people helpful.
WAYS TO ENTER FIELD	Apply to private and state employment services or direct to employers. College graduates may start as management trainees; others start as clerks and work up.	Apply to restaurant or to personnel office of chain. Watch want ads. Most start in a lower position, work their way up to manager.
CHANCE OF ADVANCEMENT	Limited. A few may become executives or start own business.	Can move to larger restaurant or better-paying position, become executive in restaurant chain, open own restaurant.
EARNINGS	In small offices: $5000–$8,000. Average: $7000–$20,000.	Managerial trainees with degrees start at $7000–$10,000. Average for experienced men: $10,000–$25,000.
SUPPLY AND DEMAND	Growing number of office managers will be needed in this competitive field.	Demand expected to increase. Competitive, but good opportunities for those with ambition, training, experience.
REFERENCES	OEK Brief No. 339	OEK Brief No. 350 WORK Brief No. 281

MARINA WORKERS

Supply gasoline, mechanical, storage service for boats. May repair engine, electrical system, hull; repaint hull; sell boats and boating equipment of all kinds; operate charter boats and sometimes serve as crew members on them; provide information about local waters and the community; help maintain navigational safety.

In more than 5000 marinas and boatyards and 1500 private yacht clubs on lakes, seacoasts, and waterways throughout U.S.

About 20,000 workers, mostly men.

High school recommended. Boating clubs, Coast Guard Power Squadron offer navigation and seamanship courses. Marine-engine manufacturers conduct courses. On-the-job training usually provided.

Liking for active outdoor work, thorough knowledge of local waters and boating skills, familiarity with boats of all kinds, mechanical skill, manual dexterity, some capability in a trade like carpentry or painting.

Apply direct to marina owners or managers. Marine engine manufacturers often have leads for those who take their training course. See *Marina Management* magazine and newspaper help-wanted ads.

Start as general helper. Later may concentrate on engine repair, hull repair and maintenance, sales. Goal of many workers is to become marina manager or owner.

Beginners: $1.60 an hour or less. Skilled workers: $5000–$10,000 a year. Marine dealers: $5000–$50,000.

Boating is very fast-growing recreation; many new water-recreation areas planned for 1970s, providing increase in employment opportunities. Heavy competition for winter jobs in warm climates.

OEK Brief No. 365
WORK Brief No. 198

MATHEMATICIANS

Analyze business and scientific problems, formulate them in mathematical terms, compute and solve. May work with electronic computers, statistics. May teach, develop mathematical theories, do pure and applied research.

Business and industry, government, educational institutions. Most are employed by manufacturing industries: aerospace and electrical equipment, computers, other office machines. Colleges and universities employ the next-largest group.

About 75,000; 10% women.

Some jobs open to those with bachelor's degree. Master's degree usually required, Ph.D. for top positions.

High level of intelligence, reasoning ability, good memory, persistence. Must be quick and accurate, present ideas clearly. Good with numbers, plane and spatial figures.

College placement offices, application to business and industrial organizations, professional contacts. Civil service examinations are given for government positions.

Excellent for those who keep up with latest developments.

Start: with bachelor's degree, $9300–$9600; with master's, $11,500–$12,000; with Ph.D., $16,000. Top: about $30,000.

Excellent opportunities. The demand is growing rapidly and is expected to continue for some time, especially for those with Ph.D.s.

OEK Brief No. 258
WORK Brief No. 200

MEATCUTTERS

Prepare and sell meat, poultry, and fish. Cut, clean, bone, trim, and grind meats. Weigh, package, and price. Display cuts and help customer make selection. Use such tools as knives, cleavers, saws, grinding and slicing machines.

Food and meat stores and markets, wholesale meat jobbers, meat-packing plants, hotels, large restaurants, and institutions throughout the U.S.

190,000 meatcutters, not counting those in packing plants. Women wrap and weigh but seldom cut meats.

High school preferred, plus 2- or 3-year apprenticeship or longer period of on-the-job training. Vocational school training helpful.

Good health, average physical strength, stamina. In some areas may need food handler's certificate Friendliness, good humor, and salesmanship helpful in smaller markets.

Apply to store or union office. Want ads, state employment agency also helpful. May start as helper, packer, delivery boy.

Can become head butcher, manager, supervisor, or open own meat market.

Journeymen: $216 a week minimum. Apprentice average: $152.

No appreciable change in number of retail meatcutters, but some growth expected at wholesale and packinghouse level. About 5000 job openings a year expected throughout the 1970s.

OEK Brief No. 192
WORK Brief No. 201

OCCUPATION	MECHANICS, AIRPLANE	MECHANICS, AUTOMOTIVE
DUTIES	Inspect, overhaul, repair, and service airplanes. May have to certify that plane is in good mechanical condition before flight. May specialize in airframe, engine, or instrument repair.	Inspect, service, and repair motor vehicles. May specialize in engine, electrical system, body, or accessories, or in work on cars, buses, trucks, tractors. Use hand and power tools. May prepare cost estimates.
WHERE EMPLOYED	Aircraft repair shops, airlines, airplane manufacturing plants, flying services, government agencies. Many work as civilians for the Air Force or Navy. Most airline mechanics work near large cities.	Service departments of auto dealers, repair shops, and garages; government agencies and companies that operate a large fleet of vehicles (taxicab and trucking companies); service stations.
NUMBER OF WORKERS	About 140,000.	More than 600,000.
EDUCATION AND TRAINING	High school diploma plus either 18–24 months in a trade or technical school or 3- or 4-year apprenticeship with scheduled airline.	High school, vocational or trade school graduation desirable. 3 or 4 years of apprenticeship or on-the-job training to become all-round skilled mechanic.
SPECIAL QUALIFICATIONS	Mechanical ability. Must have at least 18 months experience or be trade school graduate to get Federal Aviation Agency license. Must pass written and practical test.	Mechanical aptitude and skill with tools, physical stamina and good health. Willingness to work hard and honesty are desirable traits. Usually need driver's license.
WAYS TO ENTER FIELD	Armed forces experience helpful. Apply to airlines, repair shops, civil service offices. Other sources: school placement bureaus, unions, employment agencies.	Through state employment offices, unions, want ads, placement bureaus of trade schools, direct application to car dealers and repair shops.
CHANCE OF ADVANCEMENT	Chances good for skilled, responsible men. Can become lead mechanics, inspectors, foremen; can switch to higher-paying company.	Start as gas station attendant, helper, apprentice; to journeyman, specialist, foreman, service or parts manager. Can open own repair shop.
EARNINGS	Mechanics for scheduled airlines earn $800–$1100 a month. Other employers generally pay slightly less.	Beginners: $2–$2.25; may be paid on incentive system. Skilled mechanics: $4–$6.75. A good specialist can earn $14,000 or more a year.
SUPPLY AND DEMAND	Outlook good for licensed mechanics. Most openings in independent repair shops. Airline employment may increase slightly. Expect total of 6500 openings a year.	Demand increasing for men with trade school experience in auto repair. About 24,000 openings a year expected.
REFERENCES	OEK Brief No. 151 WORK Brief No. 11	OEK Brief No. 85 WORK Brief No. 34

MECHANICS, DIESEL

Maintain, repair, and rebuild diesel engines used in trucks, tractors, locomotives, and the like. Diagnose trouble, disassemble, replace or repair parts, adjust, reassemble. Use hand and machine tools and testing instruments.

Distributors of diesel equipment, bus lines, railroads, construction companies, trucking companies, shipping firms, electric power plants, garages that repair diesel equipment. Many in industrial areas.

Estimated at 85,000.

Vocational or high school plus 3–5 years on-the-job training in gas and diesel engines or 4-year apprenticeship. Trade school helpful.

Mechanical aptitude, physical strength and stamina, manual dexterity, reliability.

Trade or vocational school placement service, state employment agency, want ads, or direct application to employers. Many start as helpers, repairing gas engines.

Limited. Can become foreman, master mechanic, start own repair shop.

Journeymen: $3.70–$4.37 an hour.

Demand increasing moderately in most industries. Some competition for entry jobs; little for skilled mechanics.

OEK Brief No. 193
WORK Brief No. 92

MECHANICS, MAINTENANCE

Maintain and repair industrial machinery and equipment. Locate the source of trouble, disassemble, replace or repair defective part, adjust, reassemble. Oil, grease equipment; keep maintenance records. Use hand and power tools.

Industrial plants, especially those having a large amount of machinery. Throughout U.S., but mostly in industrialized areas.

175,000 repairmen.

High school preferred, plus several years on-the-job training or 4-year apprenticeship.

Mechanical aptitude, manual dexterity, interest in machinery, ability to follow instructions, agility, good physical condition.

Want ads, state employment service can help. Apply to union office or direct to employers. May start as helper, oiler, greaser.

Can become foreman, maintenance manager; or can switch to millwright, machinist positions.

Journeymen: $2.65–$5.09 an hour. Apprentice starts at 50%–65% of journeyman wage.

Automation creating moderate increase in demand for maintenance mechanics. Formal training will become more common.

OEK Brief No. 152
WORK Brief No. 164

MECHANICS, VENDING MACHINE

Maintain and repair electrically operated vending machines. Assemble, test, and install new machines. Determine causes of breakdowns; remove and replace parts. Periodically clean, lubricate, and adjust machines. Use hand tools; read diagrams of electrical circuits. May do some clerical work: fill out reports, keep parts inventories, order parts.

All over the country for vending machine operators, beverage companies, and vending machine manufacturers.

About 18,000.

High school diploma preferred, but not necessary. On-the-job training takes 1½–2 years.

At least 21, mechanical aptitude, manual dexterity, perseverance, thoroughness.

Want ads in newspapers and trade publications, direct application.

Usually start as helper, become mechanic trainee. May advance to senior mechanic, shop foreman, supervisor, or service manager. May start own business or go into sales.

$3–$4 an hour. Higher rates for overtime.

Moderate increase expected. Should be at least 700 job openings a year throughout the 1970s.

WORK Brief No. 333

OCCUPATION	MEDICAL ASSISTANTS (MEDICAL SECRETARIES)	MEDICAL LABORATORY ASSISTANTS
DUTIES	Greet patients; make appointments; keep office and equipment in order; type and file reports, letters, records. Take dictation and case notes, prepare patients for examination, keep books, send statements. May sterilize instruments, do some lab work.	Perform checks, counts, analyses, other laboratory procedures in bacteriology, blood banking, chemistry, hematology, parasitology, serology urinalysis. May collect specimens, prepare and stain slides, do microscopic examinations, administer electrocardiograms and basal metabolism tests, store and label plasma, clean and sterilize laboratory equipment.
WHERE EMPLOYED	Doctors' offices, government and private hospitals, clinics, medical schools, laboratories. Offices of drug manufacturers, medical suppliers, public health agencies, insurance companies.	Hospitals, medical laboratories, public health agencies, physicians' offices, industrial and pharmaceutical laboratories, veterans hospitals, armed forces, Public Health Service.
NUMBER OF WORKERS	Estimated 175,000; 98% women.	110,000; 80% are women.
EDUCATION AND TRAINING	High school graduation required. 2–4 years college or courses in junior college, business school helpful.	High school graduation plus 1 or 2 years of training in hospital laboratory school, commercial school, or junior college.
SPECIAL QUALIFICATIONS	Ability to learn medical terms and procedures. Clerical speed and accuracy, even temperament, emotional stability. Neatness, pleasant personality, resourcefulness helpful.	Good vision, manual dexterity, accuracy, ability to work under pressure and to work well with others.
WAYS TO ENTER FIELD	Newspaper want ads; school placement service; state, private, or medical employment agencies; direct application to physician or health agency.	Schools usually help graduates get first job. Applications can also be made direct to hospitals, clinics, laboratories, physicians. Check with federal Civil Service Commission, state employment service; see newspaper want ads.
CHANCE OF ADVANCEMENT	Limited in doctors' offices. To supervisory positions in larger institutions; further training may be required, however.	With additional education, may become medical technologist, then advance to supervisor in certain areas of laboratory work or to chief medical technologist in hospital.
EARNINGS	Starting salaries average $90 a week, depending on locality, training. Experienced assistants can earn well over local average for business secretaries.	Average: $4000–$8000, with large cities and West Coast generally paying the highest amounts.
SUPPLY AND DEMAND	Expect increasing need for all medical personnel. Competition not great for trained assistants. Expect 20,000 job openings a year throughout the 1970s.	Opportunities almost unlimited as population increases and medical services expand. Need at least 13,500 annually.
REFERENCES	OEK Brief No. 290 WORK Brief No. 203	OEK Brief No. 382

MERCHANT SEAMEN

Deck department: relieve helmsman and look-out, maintain decks and hull, stow and care for cargo. Engine department: clean machinery, repair and maintain equipment, chip and scale boilers, check and regulate boilers, check oil pressure and flow. Steward's department: prepare, cook, and serve food, maintain cabins.

On dry-cargo ships, tankers, barges, freighters, ferries, passenger liners, excursion steamers sailing the oceans and U.S. waterways.

31,000 unlicensed seamen (nonofficers). Majority are men; women stewardesses, waitresses, nurses on passenger liners.

No educational requirements for unlicensed seamen, who learn on the job. Shipowners associations, unions, seamen's benevolent associations offer class and correspondence courses.

Must be able to live and work in close quarters; be adaptable to long absences from home; possess seamen's papers, issued by Coast Guard.

Apply at union hiring halls in chief seaport cities; at Lake Carriers Association hiring halls in Great Lakes ports; direct to shipping companies on inland waterways. Jobs are distributed on basis of seniority and experience.

Pass Coast Guard exams to advance through departments to top unlicensed jobs: boatswain (deck crew foreman), junior engineer, chief steward. (Officers usually graduates of U.S. Merchant Marine. Coast Guard, or Naval academy)

Depend on duties. Deckman: $557 a month. Fireman: $599. Chief steward: $655. Messman: $306. Overtime adds to earnings.

Number of active oceangoing vessels about 770. So few jobs open that officers are accepting unlicensed jobs. Once established, fair chance for promotions.

OEK Brief No. 53
WORK Brief No. 207

METEOROLOGISTS

Study, analyze, and predict weather conditions. Research, practical observing, and forecasting; teaching at college or university level; administration and management of large stations or meteorological bureaus.

Federal government is largest employer. Also work for commercial airlines, public utilities, educational institutions, private weather consulting firms, insurance companies, aircraft and instrument manufacturing companies.

About 4400; 2% women.

B.S. in meteorology or related field. Advanced degrees are required for middle and top jobs.

Interest in math and science. Ability to combine seemingly unrelated facts, do abstract thinking. Logical mind, curiosity, accuracy

College placement services, Civil Service Commission, or direct application to private organizations.

Excellent. May become supervising aviation forecaster, head of weather bureau office. consultant.

Start: $8300–$14,100, depending on education and employer. Median: $15,200.

Uncrowded, growing field. Expect at least 200 job openings a year throughout the 1970s. Demand growing rapidly in industry.

OEK Brief No. 256
WORK Brief No. 209

MICROBIOLOGISTS

Study organisms of microscopic size. In medicine and public health, study causes and control of infectious diseases. May apply knowledge of microorganisms to industrial and agricultural processes or products.

Hospitals; laboratories; colleges and universities; industries such as brewing, food and drug manufacture; agricultural agencies and industries; government agencies.

About 16,000 microbiologists; at least 20% women.

Bachelor's degree with major in a biological science is the minimum. Master's required for teaching and research

Normal color vision to analyze stained slides; finger dexterity for working with small instruments; scientific interest and aptitude; precision.

College placement offices, civil service offices, state employment agency, want ads in professional journals and local newspapers, direct application.

Excellent, especially for those with advanced degree. To chief of research project, head of laboratory, production supervisor.

$6600–$8000 with bachelor's degree; $8000–$9800 with master's; $11,900–$14,200 with Ph.D. Average: $15,000.

Excellent opportunities; growing field. Greatest demand for those with graduate degrees. Little competition for able people.

OEK Brief No. 338
WORK Brief No. 210

OCCUPATION	MILLWRIGHTS	MODELS
DUTIES	Install, move, and maintain heavy industrial machinery. May also dismantle it. Plan installation, see to platform construction, unload machinery, move it into place bolt it down, assemble and install remaining components. May help in planning location of new machines.	Display products for consumers, pose for artists and photographers. Model clothing in showrooms, fashion shows, photography studios; demonstrate merchandise at trade shows or on television; make public relations films; pose for ads.
WHERE EMPLOYED	Machinery manufacturers, iron and steel industries, pulp and paper mills, auto manufacturers; construction companies; firms that contract to move and install heavy machinery. In industrial areas of U.S.	Retail stores, specialty salons in large cities; wholesale showrooms in fashion-center cities. Usually only part time for television stations, motion picture studios, mail-order houses, public relations firms, artists, photographers, sculptors.
NUMBER OF WORKERS	About 80.000, almost all men.	About 58,000; some men.
EDUCATION AND TRAINING	High school graduation recommended. 4-year apprenticeship or on-the-job training.	High school diploma. College sometimes preferred. Department store charm course or modeling school helpful.
SPECIAL QUALIFICATIONS	Mechanical aptitude; strength and agility; ability to give and carry out instructions accurately, analyze and solve problems. Must be conscientious, thorough.	Poise, grace, neat and attractive appearance, intelligence patience, personality, good speaking voice salesmanship, acting ability; should be photogenic.
WAYS TO ENTER FIELD	To become apprenticed, apply to state employment office, union or state apprenticeship council office. Can apply direct to company that employs millwrights.	Contact model agency, department store, clothing manufacturer, specialty store, television studio. Model agencies usually charge a 10%–25% fee.
CHANCE OF ADVANCEMENT	May become maintenance supervisor, shop foreman, installation mechanic; switch to a related field of work.	Depends largely on seeking own appointments. Photographers' models get top pay, prestige. May go into fashion advertising, fashion-show production, model-bureau ownership.
EARNINGS	Vary throughout U.S.: $3.21–$4.75 an hour. Contract millwrights get top wages. Apprentices start at 50% of journeyman rate.	Start: $65–$100 a week. Experienced: $100–$125. Top: $40 000 a year or more. Photographers' models: $25–$50 an hour, but might work only a few hours a week.
SUPPLY AND DEMAND	Excellent opportunities. Little competition for jobs; 31,000 openings a year.	Extremely competitive Photographers' models often replaced after only 5 years. Supply is much greater than the demand. Only about 2000 job openings a year.
REFERENCES	OEK Brief No. 222 WORK Brief No. 211	OEK Brief No. 167 WORK Brief No. 213

MUSEUM WORKERS	MUSICIANS	NURSERYMEN AND LANDSCAPERS
Work generally in one of three areas: exhibition, education, research. May plan or help build exhibits; lecture do research. write; act as instructor-guide; work in museum administration.	Play one or more musical instruments, solo or in orchestra, band, combo. Usually specialize in either classical or popular music. May teach, write, and arrange music; sing, accompany soloist.	Nurserymen select, propagate, and tend plants; perhaps sell, give advice about them. Landscapers design and supervise landscaping of buildings, parks, playgrounds, housing projects, industrial sites, highways, and the like.
In about 5000 museums in the U.S. and Canada.	Orchestras, bands, nightclubs, theaters, TV and motion picture studios, churches, schools, recording companies. Some play at parties, receptions, dances, dinners. Mostly in cities.	Nurserymen work in wholesale or retail nurseries, greenhouses, and garden centers. Landscapers may work for nurserymen, landscape contractors, civic or government agencies.
Undetermined. Field is small; fewer than 30,000 professionals.	About 210,000 musicians and music teachers.	More than 45,000 full-time workers. Some women, especially in sales and tending.
Vary with job. Most curators have Ph.D. Instructor-guides may have high school only.	No definite requirements, but many take private lessons, attend music school. Need bachelor's degree for teaching.	High school is sufficient for some jobs. On-the-job training is usually given. College courses needed for advanced positions.
Interest in art, science, history, education. Be attentive to details; work without close supervision; get along with others.	Musical aptitude, love of music, perseverance. patience, ambition, willingness to work hard. Individuality, strong personality, attractive appearance are helpful. Musicians' union membership required.	Love for and knowledge of plants, sense of beauty and proportion, willingness to do manual labor and outdoor work, manual dexterity, good coordination, patience.
Direct application to museum; personal contact.	May start in school band or orchestra, or form combo with fellow students, friends. Personal contacts, union office, auditions, direct application.	Can begin as a laborer. State employment agency, want ads may list available jobs. College horticultural departments help place graduates.
Promotion often slow. Assistant curators can be promoted to chiefs, then to museum directors.	Limited. Best jobs go to those with talent, persistence.	Ability and experience may lead to becoming foreman or starting a business of one's own.
Vary with job. Curators: $5000–$19,000; median, $9271. Directors: to $40,000: average $15,912.	Players in big symphonies: $5100–$16,500 for season; ensembles, $200 a concert. Bands: $60–$300.	Vary greatly with skills, responsibility, experience, geographic area. Beginners: $1.60–$2.50 an hour. Experienced: $3–$6 an hour.
Keen competition, little turnover. But museums are growing in popularity; expect many beginning jobs in small museums throughout the 1970s.	Number of musicians growing, but tremendous competition in all fields except teaching.	Landscaping and nursery business flourishing. Openings at all levels. Greatest demand for college graduates. Little competition.
OEK Brief No. 219 WORK Brief No. 215	OEK Brief No. 133 WORK Brief No. 216	OEK Brief No. 166 WORK Brief No. 220

OCCUPATION	NURSES, PRACTICAL	NURSES, PUBLIC HEALTH
DUTIES	See to patients' well-being. Take temperature, pulse rate, and blood pressure, change dressings, keep records. May give medication and injections. In private-duty nursing, may have some housekeeping duties.	Care for patients in clinics or in their homes; give first-aid treatment or periodic nursing care, demonstrate diet plans to groups of patients or families, arrange for immunizations. May work in community health education programs in schools. May teach.
WHERE EMPLOYED	Hospitals, public health agencies, doctors' offices, sanitariums, industries, schools, summer camps, children's or old people's or nursing homes. Private-duty nursing in hospital or patient's home	Local health departments, private agencies such as visiting nurse associations, public school systems, business and industry, several government agencies.
NUMBER OF WORKERS	About 370,000; 5% men.	More than 50,000. Most are women.
EDUCATION AND TRAINING	Eighth-grade education minimum, high school desirable. Then 12–18-month course in approved public or private school.	Bachelor's degree in nursing.
SPECIAL QUALIFICATIONS	After graduation, pass state exam for license. Should have liking for and desire to help people. Common sense, maturity, adaptability, reliability, warmth, patience, tolerance cheerfulness.	Interest in people, desire to care for sick and injured, dependability, good judgment, patience good physical and mental health. Must pass state board examination to be licensed as a registered nurse.
WAYS TO ENTER FIELD	Approved schools of practical nursing. Civil Service Commission, nurse placement agencies, and newspaper want ads all list available jobs. Apply direct to hospitals, other institutions.	Direct application to nursing agencies, local health departments, school systems, large industrial plants, Army Nurse Corps, Veterans Administration hospitals. Check want ads in professional nursing journals.
CHANCE OF ADVANCEMENT	Limited Experience and further training necessary to become a professional nurse.	Some advance to supervisory positions. Can go into teaching, research, or administration.
EARNINGS	Start about $110 a week. Private-duty pay depends on hours, duties, locality; range $15–$30 a day.	Average salaries: private agencies, about $7986, local government agencies, $8477. Top jobs: $20,000 or more.
SUPPLY AND DEMAND	Little competition. The demand is great and expected to grow as long as the shortage of professional nurses continues. Can use 58,000 more practical nurses a year.	Expect to need 100,000 public health nurses by early 1970s. Many opportunities for men.
REFERENCES	OEK Brief No. 119 WORK Brief No. 185	OEK Brief No. 394 WORK Brief No. 265

NURSES, REGISTERED

Provide patients with nursing care either directly or by supervising other nurses. May specialize as hospital nurse, public health nurse, private-duty nurse, office nurse, occupational health nurse, educator.

Hospitals, clinics, public health agencies, industries, nursing schools, doctors' offices, research organizations, nursing homes, sanitariums, armed forces. Peace Corps; private duty in hospital or patient's home.

About 700,000; 98% women.

Junior college, 2 years; or hospital nursing school, usually 3 years; or college 4 or 5. Graduate training for top positions.

High school graduation in top half or third of class recommended for admittance to nursing school. After graduation from training, must pass state board exam to obtain license.

Apply directly to hospital, watch want ads, submit qualifications to a professional nursing registry. American Nurses' Association has a placement service.

Good. May specialize or, with experience and possibly further education, get supervisory, administrative, teaching position.

Average: $7900–$9700 a year.

Excellent opportunities. The demand much greater than the supply. Critical shortage of administrators, educators. 70,000 openings a year. Men encouraged.

OEK Brief No. 70
WORK Brief No. 279

OCEANOGRAPHERS

Study the sea with respect to structure; composition; plant, animal, and chemical content. May specialize in physical, geological, geophysical, chemical, or biological aspects. Make voyages, do research in labs, teach.

Colleges and universities employ the largest number for teaching and research. Others work for government agencies, research laboratories, and in industry.

About 5400.

About 60% of all oceanographers have graduate degrees. Ph.D essential to progress in this field.

Above-average intelligence. aptitude and interest in science inquisitive mind, ability to work without supervision, accuracy, good health, liking for life aboard ship.

College placement bureaus, direct application to industries, Civil Service Commission, recommendation of professors or others in the field.

Can become head of research project, full professor, administrator. Advancement may be slow.

Median start with Ph.D.: $12,000. Experienced, median: $14,900. With federal government: start, $8292–$14,192; top, $23,000 or more.

Opportunities are excellent, especially for those with Ph.D About 300 openings a year; little competition.

OEK Brief No. 188
WORK Brief No. 222

OFFICE MACHINE OPERATORS

Operate office machines used for calculating, recording, writing, billing, addressing, mailing, duplicating, coding, sorting, and the like. Usually operate one kind of machine, such as keypunch, autotype billing.

Government agencies, manufacturing companies, banks, insurance companies, wholesale and retail businesses, other organizations throughout U.S.

About 365,000; more than 25% men.

High school diploma usually required. Business school training helpful. A few days to several weeks on-the-job training given.

Finger dexterity, good eye-hand coordination, accuracy, good vision. Mechanical ability helpful for those who operate larger machines. Skill on several machines desirable.

Apply to prospective employers. Watch want ads; try state, private employment agencies. Civil service offices, business school placement services list openings.

Can become operator of more complex machine; supervisor; possibly office manager.

Average: $4600–$7800 a year, depending on machine and experience. Tabulating machine operators earn most.

One of the fastest-growing clerical occupations with about 21,000 openings annually. Average competition for the better-paying jobs.

OEK Brief No. 154
WORK Brief No. 223

OCCUPATION	OPHTHALMOLOGISTS	OPTICIANS AND OPTICAL MECHANICS
DUTIES	Specialize in eye diseases or injuries. Perform eye surgery, prescribe drugs or other treatments and lenses. Give eye examinations.	Dispensing opticians receive prescription, measure patient for width of glasses and position of lenses, show frames, write order, adjust finished glasses to wearer. Optical mechanics grind, cut, polish, and mount lenses in frames.
WHERE EMPLOYED	In private practice, clinics, hospitals; mainly in urban areas.	Wholesale and retail optical firms throughout U.S., especially in larger cities and industrial areas. In smaller towns, most opportunities in retail establishments.
NUMBER OF WORKERS	About 10,200.	About 11,000 dispensing opticians and 15,000 optical mechanics; some women.
EDUCATION AND TRAINING	2, 3, or 4 years college, plus 4 years medical school, 1 year internship, and 3–4 years residency in ophthalmology.	High school graduation. 2 years college or vocational-school training helpful. Usually 4- or 5-year apprenticeship.
SPECIAL QUALIFICATIONS	Scientific aptitude and ability, manual dexterity, intelligence, perseverance, stamina, responsibility. Must pass exam for state license.	May need state license. Finger dexterity, some mechanical ability, patience, accuracy, liking for precision work. Dispensing opticians should be personable.
WAYS TO ENTER FIELD	Can start own practice or be assistant to established doctor and later buy practice. May hear of need through personal contact with opticians and drug salesmen.	Direct application to optical company or laboratory. Want ads or employment agencies list openings. Colleges and vocational schools have placement offices for graduates.
CHANCE OF ADVANCEMENT	May advance by building reputation and increasing size of practice; becoming hospital chief, university professor, research specialist.	Optical mechanic to dispensing optician, contact-lens fitter, manager. Can become foreman, superintendent; open own shop.
EARNINGS	First-year earnings usually low. After practice is established, may average $25,000–$50,000 a year.	Mechanics: beginners, $1.94–$2.25 an hour; experienced, $2.50–$4.25. Opticians: $3.50–$7.50.
SUPPLY AND DEMAND	Good opportunities but some competition for medical school openings.	Expect moderate increase in employment of opticians. Little change in need for optical mechanics. Women encouraged.
REFERENCES	OEK Brief No. 146 WORK Brief No. 226	OEK Brief No. 86 WORK Brief Nos. 227, 228

OPTOMETRISTS

Examine and test eyes; prescribe glasses, contact lenses, or eye exercises. Do not prescribe or use drugs or perform surgery. Some teach; do research; specialize in children, the nearly blind, industrial lighting, relation of sight to accidents.

Primarily in private practice. Also in schools, clinics, hospitals, health agencies, armed forces. May teach or do research in universities, work for optical manufacturers, government agencies.

About 18,000; 4% women.

2 years preoptometry training in college plus 4 years in accredited optometry school. Additional training to specialize.

Must obtain license by passing state exam after graduation. Should have aptitude for science, math, mechanics. Finger dexterity, accuracy, patience, tact, good personality helpful.

Begin as assistant to gain experience and earn enough to start own practice. Many begin private practice just after graduation or buy established one. Good opportunities in small cities, new communities.

Make success of own business. Depends largely on ability and location.

New graduates, salaried: $10,000–$15,000. In own practice: very low first few years; after some experience, $15,000–$30,000.

Demand greater than supply, and will continue to increase with population. Many areas have little or no competition. At least 800 openings a year.

OEK Brief No. 34
WORK Brief No. 229

PAINTERS, PRODUCTION

Use spray gun or brush to apply paint or other finish to surface of manufactured items. Some use dipping tank, tumbling barrels, or semiautomatic paint-spraying machines. May use masking tape, mix paint, clean equipment.

In almost every plant that manufactures products or components made of wood or metal. Most work in industrial areas.

About 115,000; 15% women.

No specific educational requirements. Several weeks of on-the-job training usually given.

Good health, good eyesight, physical stamina, ability to stand paint fumes.

Apply direct to manufacturing plant. Watch want ads; visit state employment office

Poor. A few may become foremen, inspectors.

$2.86–$4.32 an hour.

Employment of these painters expected to remain relatively stable. Need 3700 replacements a year.

WORK Brief No. 258

PAINTERS AND PAPERHANGERS

Prepare surface by removing old paint or paper, smoothing, cleaning, priming, or sizing. Painters mix and apply paint or similar coating. Paperhangers measure cut, paste, and apply wall covering. Use brushes, rollers, spray guns, other hand tools.

With painting and decorating contractors who specialize in building construction, maintenance, and alterations. Some opportunities in hotels, schools, office buildings, factories, other large buildings, shipyards, government agencies.

About 422,000 painters and paperhangers; few women.

High school desirable. Formal 3-year apprenticeship recommended over informal training as a helper.

Manual dexterity, good physical condition, agility, color sense. Neatness and reliability helpful.

For apprenticeship, apply to local union office or joint apprenticeship council. For a job as a helper, apply directly to a contractor.

Can advance to foreman, estimator for contractor, superintendent, or start own contracting firm.

Average: about $5 an hour. Helpers earn about half as much.

Replacement needs will continue to create many openings, especially for painters. Expect 22,000 job openings a year throughout the 1970s.

OEK Brief No. 87
WORK Brief No. 230

OCCUPATION	PARKING ATTENDANTS	PEDIATRICIANS
DUTIES	Park customers' cars in parking lots and garages. Give customer claim check; may accept payment and make change, wipe windshield and clean interior of car.	Diagnose, treat, prevent organic illness of children from infancy through adolescence. Supervise child's growth and development by means of routine health exams. May study child's emotional and psychological life.
WHERE EMPLOYED	Mostly in municipal and private parking lots and garages. Some work in lots run by hotels and motels, restaurants, nightclubs, apartment buildings, stores, and clubs. Throughout U.S., especially in cities.	Most are in private practice. Others work in hospitals, clinics, public health agencies, medical schools, research foundations, pharmaceutical firms, and the armed forces.
NUMBER OF WORKERS	About 50,000 full-time auto service and parking attendants; 2% women.	About 14,000; 15% women.
EDUCATION AND TRAINING	High school diploma not required, but preferred in many lots and garages.	2 to 4 years college plus 4 years medical school, 1 year internship, and 2–4 years residency in pediatrics or a subspecialty.
SPECIAL QUALIFICATIONS	Driver's license required. Must know how to operate all makes of cars. Good vision, quick reflexes. Courtesy and caution helpful. May need special license.	Liking for and understanding of children, scientific aptitude, emotional maturity, intelligence. stamina, perseverance, tact, responsibility, integrity, sense of humor. Must pass state exam for state license.
WAYS TO ENTER FIELD	Apply to parking lot or garage. Newspaper want ads and state employment service can help. Part-time work available.	Can start own practice or be assistant to established doctor and later buy practice Can apply direct to hospitals, clinics, and the like.
CHANCE OF ADVANCEMENT	Poor. In some cases attendants can advance to manager.	In private practice. income increases as doctor acquires reputation. In other areas, regular channels of advancement.
EARNINGS	Wages $1.60–$3 an hour, not counting tips, which may make up a large part of total earnings.	Median: $30,000–$37,500 a year.
SUPPLY AND DEMAND	Increase in cars and parking lots may be offset by automated parking. Demand should remain fairly constant.	In great demand, especially in low-income areas.
REFERENCES	OEK Brief No. 341	OEK Brief No. 375 WORK Brief No. 233

PERSONNEL WORKERS

Recruit, screen, hire new employees. May administer or develop training programs; evaluate for promotions, pay raises; deal with job problems; establish policies. Develop job classifications, pay scales, benefits. Keep records.

Almost every sizable industrial, business, government, and nonprofit organization has one or more personnel workers. More than half are in industry.

Over 160,000 in personnel and related fields; 25% women.

College degree often minimum. Master's or doctor's degree may be required for top jobs. In-service training common.

Should be objective, patient, emotionally stable, personable, good judge of character, tactful, discreet. Sound judgment, leadership qualities, common sense are important.

School placement services, state or private employment agencies, want ads; direct application to companies, civil service offices. May start as trainee, assistant.

Good. To training director, job analyst, personnel manager, industrial relations director, vice-president in charge of personnel.

Starting salaries, with bachelor's degree, average $7600. Experienced: $14,000–$19,000, depending on size of the company.

Competitive, but good potential for those with a college degree. Field will expand with industry and population, opening about 9100 jobs each year.

OEK Brief No. 134
WORK Brief No. 234

PEST CONTROL OPERATORS

Inspect premises for type of pest, places of entry, nest locations; remove dead pests. Select appropriate control method. Operate hand or mechanical sprayer to spray or dust chemical; set out bait or traps. Suggest housekeeping or maintenance methods to aid control. May accept payment for service, turn in money to employer, keep records.

With 5000 pest control contractors and with local government agencies, armed forces, food processors, baking companies, food packers or shippers.

More than 50,000; few women.

High school diploma. Some short courses and 2-year technical courses available. Employers provide brief training period, then assign beginner to a route with experienced man.

Mechancial aptitude, agility. No squeamishness; no allergy to chemicals used in work. Friendly, courteous, patient attitude toward customers; responsibleness. Have state driver's license.

Apply to pest control companies. Look for ads in help-wanted columns of newspapers and *Pest Control* magazine. Check with state and private employment agencies.

Somewhat limited. May become foreman, route manager, service manager if company is large enough. May concentrate on building sales. Some start own business, perhaps specializing in termite control, bird management, fumigation.

Beginners: $90–$110 a week. Experienced: $150–$200.

Lively demand for qualified personnel; field is generally uncrowded. Men with a little experience or technical knowledge will find excellent opportunities.

OEK Brief No. 362
WORK Brief No. 235

PHARMACISTS

Fill prescriptions, compound and dispense drugs, sell medicines and other merchandise, keep records. May supervise drugstore employees, manage own business, sell and promote drugs for manufacturers, teach, do research.

Most either own or are employed in retail drugstore. Others work for drug manufacturers and wholesalers, hospitals, government agencies, colleges of pharmacy.

More than 129,000; 10% women.

At least 5 years of college, including 3 or more in pharmacy school, plus 1 year in-service training.

Scientific aptitude, accuracy, honesty, business sense, friendliness, dependability. Must pass state exam to get license.

Apply to personnel office of drugstore chain or directly to independent stores. Watch want ads. College placement service usually helpful.

Good. Can become store manager, go into distribution or sales, open own drugstore.

Starting salaries: $150–$200 a week. Experienced: to $15,000.

Gradual increase in pharmacists expected; little competition for openings. Always a need for those with graduate degrees. Project about 5100 openings a year.

OEK Brief No. 74
WORK Brief No. 237

OCCUPATION	PHARMACOLOGISTS	PHOTOGRAPHERS
DUTIES	Determine effects of drugs on life processes; discover and develop new or improved chemical compounds for certain desired effects on organisms; conduct tests on animals to determine physiological effects of drugs, gases, dusts, poisons, and chemicals on tissues and organs, correlate these findings with medical data on humans. May teach, write, do research.	Photograph people, places, and things, using a variety of cameras, lenses, film, and other equipment. May develop, enlarge, print photos. May specialize as studio, industrial, press photographer.
WHERE EMPLOYED	Colleges, universities, hospitals, government agencies, pharmaceutical and chemical manufacturers, privately financed research organizations or foundations.	Portrait and commercial photographic studios, industrial companies, newspapers and magazines, government agencies, camera shops and stores, organizations. Many do freelance work.
NUMBER OF WORKERS	6000–8000; less than 5% women.	About 65,000 full-time photographers; 12% women.
EDUCATION AND TRAINING	Master's degree is barely adequate for beginning jobs. Advancement always requires more education: Ph.D. or degree in medicine, veterinary medicine, or dentistry.	High school plus 2 or 3 years in art, trade, technical school, or on-the-job training. College or junior college degree desirable.
SPECIAL QUALIFICATIONS	Curiosity about living things, keen powers of observation, logical thought processes, patience, ability to communicate findings simply and clearly in writing and speaking.	Sense of color and form, artistic ability, manual dexterity, knowledge of photographic techniques. In some specialties imagination, business sense, ability to judge news value.
WAYS TO ENTER FIELD	Campus interviews, college placement service, recommendation of professors; direct application to chemical and pharmaceutical manufacturers and other private employers; civil service applications.	School placement service, state employment agencies, want ads helpful. Apply to studio, camera shop, other employer. May start as assistant or technician.
CHANCE OF ADVANCEMENT	With experience and advanced education, may become professor, researcher, administrator in various capacities. Some serve as consultants, write, head own business.	Fair chance to open own studio, free-lance.
EARNINGS	Beginners: $8000–$12,000 a year. Experienced: median, $12,000–$20,000; upper level, $20,000–$30,000.	Start: $125–$140 a week. Experienced: $165–$290. Top: $20.000 for studio, free-lance photographers.
SUPPLY AND DEMAND	Some opportunity for those with master's degree who plan to continue graduate study. Heavy demand for men and women with doctorates, especially for teaching. Supply far short of need.	Demand increasing. Keen competition; little turnover in newspaper work. Total openings, about 200 annually.
REFERENCES	OEK Brief No. 380	OEK Brief Nos. 35, 264 WORK Brief Nos. 71, 254

PHYSICIANS

Prevent, diagnose, treat illnesses, aid patient rehabilitation. May be general practitioner; specialize in such areas as surgery, pediatrics, obstetrics, gynecology, internal medicine. May teach, do medical research.

Most are in private practice. Others work in hospitals, clinics, public health agencies, medical schools, research foundations, medical associations, and the armed forces.

About 305,000: 7% women.

3 or 4 years college plus 4 years medical school and at least 1-year internship. Specialists need 2–5 year residency in addition.

Intelligence, scientific aptitude liking for people, perseverance, stamina, tact, responsibility, integrity, emotional stability. Must pass exam for state license.

Can start own practice or be assistant to established doctor and later buy practice. Can apply direct to hospitals, clinics, and the like.

In private practice, income increases as doctor acquires reputation. In other areas, regular channels of advancement.

In private practice: average $35,000 a year. Many earn far more.

Shortage of doctors expected to continue as demand increases. Stiff competition for medical school admission.

OEK Brief No. 136
WORK Brief Nos. 233, 242, 313

PHYSICISTS

Study and investigate matter, energy, and relation between them. Do pure or applied research. May specialize in mechanics, optics, thermodynamics, acoustics, nuclear physics, electronics, solid-state physics, theoretical physics. May teach, write.

Many work in private industry, especially in the electronics and aerospace industries. Others work for colleges and universities, government agencies, research laboratories.

About 48,000; 3% women.

B.S. is minimum requirement. For research and college teaching, graduate degree (usually Ph.D.) required.

Above-average intelligence. highly inquisitive mind, accuracy, abstract reasoning ability, imagination, persistence acute observation.

On-campus interviews, placement bureaus, recommendation of graduate school professor, want ads in newspapers, notices in professional journals.

Good. Can direct own research project, obtain supervisory or administrative position, become consultant, write extensively.

Start: $9200–$16,200, depending on education. Top: $30,000 or more. Pay highest in industry, lowest in teaching.

Today there are more physicists than jobs available. Oversupply expected to last until 1980. Some opportunities in high school and junior college teaching.

OEK Brief No. 75
WORK Brief No. 243

PLASTERERS

Apply several coats of plaster to unfinished walls and ceilings with trowel, smooth with straight-edge tools, finish. May apply stucco or cement-lime finish to outsides of buildings; form ornamental designs; operate plaster-spraying machines.

Most work for plastering and lathing contractors in building construction industry; some self-employed.

About 35,000, almost all men.

High school diploma plus 3- or 4-year apprenticeship. Many learn the trade through on-the-job training.

Good health and physical stamina, manual dexterity, agility. May have to pass practical exam for journeyman status.

Apply to union local or to plastering contractor. State employment service may be helpful.

Limited. May become foreman, estimator. Many are self-employed; a few can become contractors.

Union minimum for journeymen: $5.50 an hour. Apprentices start at 45% of journeyman wage.

Moderate increase in employment expected. About 1000 openings a year. Average competition for apprenticeships.

OEK Brief No. 227
WORK Brief No. 245

OCCUPATION	PLUMBERS AND PIPEFITTERS	PODIATRISTS
DUTIES	Install, alter, and repair pipe systems that carry water, gas, steam, waste matter, and air. Cut, bend, thread, and connect pipe; test for leaks. Use wrenches, other hand tools, power tools. May install plumbing fixtures.	Diagnose and treat diseases and deformities of the feet. Perform foot surgery, use drugs and physical therapy, prescribe proper shoes, fit (sometimes make) corrective devices. Take X-rays, perform blood and other tests, refer patients to medical doctors as needed. May specialize; may teach, write.
WHERE EMPLOYED	Most work for plumbing and pipefitting contractors. Others work for public utilities, government agencies, industrial concerns. Many are self-employed. Throughout U.S., especially in growing residential and industrial areas.	Most are in private practice. A few work in hospitals, podiatry colleges, for the Veterans Administration, or as commissioned officers in the armed forces.
NUMBER OF WORKERS	About 350,000, almost all men.	About 8500.
EDUCATION AND TRAINING	High school diploma desirable plus 5-year formal apprenticeship. Some learn through on-the-job training.	At least 2 years of college plus 4 years in one of the five podiatry colleges in U.S. Some states require 1-year internship. Specialization requires additional education and practice.
SPECIAL QUALIFICATIONS	Mechanical aptitude, manual dexterity, physical stamina, accuracy, responsibility. Knowledge of basic math and science May have to pass exam for plumbing license.	Scientific aptitude, manual dexterity. Ability to get along well with people and gain satisfaction in serving them. Tact, honesty, good business sense. Ability to pass state board exam for license.
WAYS TO ENTER FIELD	Apply to union local, local joint apprenticeship committee, or plumbing contractor.	Most newly licensed podiatrists open own practice. Some buy established practice, go into partnership with another doctor, or work for another doctor on salaried basis. Apply to podiatry schools for teaching positions, to armed forces branch for commission.
CHANCE OF ADVANCEMENT	Can become master plumber or pipefitter, foreman, inspector, estimator; start own business as a contractor.	Most advancement comes in attracting more patients and enlarging practice as a result of good reputation. Adding teaching, writing to private practice is advancement for some.
EARNINGS	Journeymen: $5–$9.42. Apprentices usually start at 63% of journeyman wage.	Range: $6000–$45,000. Incomes are generally highest in larger cities.
SUPPLY AND DEMAND	About 20,000 openings a year in these large and growing occupations, though competition for apprenticeships may be keen.	Field not crowded. Expect 250 openings a year throughout the 1970s. Women encouraged.
REFERENCES	OEK Brief No. 88 WORK Brief No. 246	OEK Brief No. 243 WORK Brief No. 247

POLICEMEN AND POLICEWOMEN

Enforce laws; protect citizens and property; investigate crimes, suspicious actions, complaints, accidents; prevent crime; apprehend criminals. Keep order in emergencies; direct traffic; give first aid.

City, town, county, and state government agencies throughout U.S.

About 350,000 city and town policemen; 14,000 policewomen.

Usually high school plus 2 weeks to several months in police school. College sometimes required.

Physical strength and courage, stamina, good health. Honesty, emotional stability, alertness. Must pass written, oral, physical exams and character check. U.S. citizen.

Apply to headquarters of state, county, or local police department.

Fair. Patrolmen or officers to sergeant, lieutenant, captain, usually based on department-wide tests. Those with college training have best chance. Top job, chief or superintendent, usually by appointment, often from the ranks.

Rookies: $4800–$9000. Experienced patrolmen: $10,000. Chiefs: to $30,000. Highest salaries in big cities.

Demand rapidly increasing for policemen and policewomen, but competition may be very keen for advancement and for the more than 17,000 openings each year.

OEK Brief Nos. 54, 107
WORK Brief Nos. 248, 249

POLITICAL SCIENTISTS

Study government—what it is and does, how it operates, how it affects the governed—at every level; analyze patterns, sources of political power; study domestic, foreign affairs. Collect facts, analyze them, work into system of knowledge. May specialize in American government, international relations. Most teach, write; may lecture, do consulting work.

In almost every college and university in U.S. Also in government—75% in Washington, others in large cities, state capitals, overseas. A few in research bureaus, civic and taxpayers associations, large business firms.

About 13,000; 8% women.

Master's degree in political science, international relations, or public administration; doctor's degree highly desirable

Intense curiosity about all aspects of government, interest in history, sound judgment, cooperative attitude in teamwork.

Recommendations by professors, campus interviews, direct application to colleges for teaching positions. Contact federal and state civil service offices about government jobs, check with American Political Science Association.

College instructors may be promoted to assistant professor, associate professor, full professor. Ability, experience. degree of responsibility, and seniority may qualify civil service employees for higher grade and salary.

Start: $8000–$10,500, depending on degree. Top: $25,000 or more. Teachers add to income by speaking, writing, research.

Expect continued increase in demand for both teachers and government employees; about 800 openings a year.

OEK Brief No. 366
WORK Brief No. 250

POULTRYMEN

Raise poultry for eggs or meat. Buy or hatch chicks. Feed and water flock, probably mechanically. Arrange for proper housing and cleanliness, light, heat, ventilation. Gather eggs, cull unproductive layers from flock. Arrange marketing of products. Keep detailed records. May do research, administrative work, teaching, writing.

Poultry farms throughout U.S., especially in Georgia, Virginia, Maryland, Delaware, Maine, Iowa, Minnesota, California, New York. Trained poultrymen also sought by federal and state government agencies, feed processors, hatcheries.

About 200,000 commercial poultry farms. Many are one-man operations.

No specific requirements, but an agricultural college education is a distinct advantage. University correspondence or extension courses helpful. Future Farmers or 4-H poultry projects can be helpful.

Physical stamina, mechanical ability, inclination toward neatness, attentiveness to detail. Must have capital or be able to borrow $20,000 or more to start own business.

Apply direct to poultry farms. Vacation and afterschool work may lead to full-time employment. Poultry associations, county extension service may provide leads.

Most poultrymen want to own their own business and strive to enlarge it. Some manage farms for individuals, feed companies, dairies, experimental or research agencies. Some find advancement in administrative work.

Depend on many factors: size of flock, type of production, individual ability—and luck. May range from $2000–$20,000 and fluctuate by year.

Demand for college graduates with poultry-raising background exceeds supply by nearly 5 to 1. Abundant opportunities with government agencies, hatcheries, feed processors.

OEK Brief No. 47
WORK Brief No. 252

OCCUPATION	POWER TRUCK OPERATORS	PRINTING PRESSMEN
DUTIES	Operate self-powered truck with lifting mechanism to move heavy materials. Operate controls to start, stop, move truck; control lifting mechanism and attachments. May do some manual loading and unloading, keep records of materials moved, maintain truck in good working condition by cleaning, oiling, checking batteries, making simple adjustments.	Set up, adjust, and operate letterpress, gravure, and offset printing presses. Clean and adjust press, insert form or plate, run sample copies, check printed copies, make needed adjustments, keep press in working condition.
WHERE EMPLOYED	Manufacturing plants, warehouses, supply depots, dock terminals, mines, other places where quantities of materials must be moved. Throughout U.S., but half the total workers are in North Central states.	Commercial printing plants, printshops of book, newspaper, and magazine publishers. Many work in large cities.
NUMBER OF WORKERS	About 200,000 men.	About 85,000 pressmen and plate printers; 4% women.
EDUCATION AND TRAINING	No specified educational requirements. A few large companies have formal training programs. Most train on the job; driver can learn to operate truck in a few days; several weeks to learn other details.	High school plus 2–5 years of apprenticeship or informal on-the-job training. Trade school training helpful.
SPECIAL QUALIFICATIONS	Mechanical aptitude, excellent coordination, ability to judge distances and space relationships. May have to pass physical exam.	Mechanical ability, manual dexterity, good vision (including color), physical stamina, alertness.
WAYS TO ENTER FIELD	Check want ads, inquire at state employment service and local union office. Apply direct to factories, warehouses, supply yards, dock terminals, and the like.	Apply to printing shops or plants, union offices. Trade school placement bureau may be helpful. Watch want ads, contact state employment service. May start as helper, assistant.
CHANCE OF ADVANCEMENT	Opportunities for advancement depend on size of plant. May become materials-movement foreman or supervisor.	Advance to more complicated press. Some chance to become foreman, plant manager, open own printshop.
EARNINGS	Average: about $3 an hour. Pay depends on size and location of plant.	Average: journeymen, $4.94; assistants, $4.26.
SUPPLY AND DEMAND	Foresee moderate increase in demand, at least until 1980. Expect fair amount of competition for the 5100 job openings a year.	Demand increasing moderately. About 2400 openings annually. Some competition for apprenticeships.
REFERENCES	OEK Brief No. 344 WORK Brief No. 253	OEK Brief No. 90 WORK Brief No. 255

PROBATION AND PAROLE OFFICERS

Assist probationers, parolees, juvenile offenders in readjustment to society. Make investigations, submit reports to courts on activities of clients; counsel clients, may help find jobs, direct them to other community services. May arrange for adoptions, provide marriage counseling, collect court-ordered payments for support of families.

Federal, state, county, and city governments throughout U.S.

17,000 full-time probation and parole officers.

Bachelor's degree in social sciences. Graduate study and a year of casework experience in a correctional institution, social agency, or similar organization are desirable.

Deep concern for people, patience, perseverance, emotional maturity and stability, common sense, personal integrity, self-discipline. Thorough knowledge of community in which employed.

Check with federal and state civil service agencies about openings and competitive exams for parole jobs; with county and city agencies for probation jobs. National Council on Crime and Delinquency lists opportunities in its journal.

Most advancement will require graduate study. Can move to casework supervisor, chief probation or parole officer, director of the parole or probation department. Some shift to teaching, research work.

Start: $6500–$9950. Experienced: to $20,000. Directors and chiefs: $12,000–$35,000.

Most probation and parole departments are understaffed. Opportunities virtually unlimited for qualified men and women to fill acute shortage that is expected to continue indefinitely.

OEK Brief No. 289
WORK Brief No. 256

PRODUCT DEMONSTRATORS

Show how a product, especially a new one, is used or prepared, as a method of advertising and selling. May set up display, prepare a product such as food, pass out samples or literature, demonstrate use or operation, offer product to observers for inspection or trial use, make oral or written surveys among onlookers, give sales talk, answer questions, handle sales.

Department stores and supermarkets, food and industrial trade shows and conventions throughout U.S. Assigned to locations by employing manufacturer.

Undetermined. Great majority are women.

High school education. Some jobs require technical or professional education or experience. Manufacturers usually train or send demonstrators out with experienced workers. Sales experience helpful.

Pleasing personality, pleasant speaking voice, neat appearance; poise, self-confidence, enthusiasm for product. Ability to speak before a group and to approach people. Physical stamina to stand for several hours consecutively.

Apply to local demonstrators union or to manufacturers whose products lend themselves effectively to demonstration. Watch newspaper want ads; check with state employment service.

Limited for those who work on temporary or part-time basis. Experienced and full-time people get most interesting assignments and best pay. Some find opportunities in sales, advertising, public relations.

Temporary or part-time workers: $16–$25 a day. Considerable variation in salary for full-time demonstrators.

Because direct personal approach seems very effective for sales promotion, more companies are expected to hire and train full-time demonstrators.

OEK Brief No. 343
WORK Brief No. 257

PROFESSIONAL ATHLETES

Play baseball, football, basketball, hockey as a team member in a league; play tennis or golf, bowl, box, or wrestle in competition before paying audiences.

Minor, major league baseball teams; professional football, basketball, hockey teams; individual competition in tennis, golf, bowling, boxing, wrestling, often sponsored by club, business organization, or individual.

Relatively few (under 3000) professionals in any sport. Mostly men.

High school, college helpful for most sports and for other employment when athletic career is ended. Intensive coaching and practice. Play on neighborhood, school teams; enter amateur tournaments.

Excellent health, good muscle coordination, speed, alertness, depth and distance perception; fierce desire to excel, strong liking for competition.

Baseball hopefuls can apply direct to team. Football, basketball, baseball players usually recruited by scouts who watch college and high school athletes and invite exceptional players to try out professionally. Individual route: usually by winning local and national amateur competitions.

Be a leader and winner, resulting in bigger earnings. Few can be successful professional athletes after age 35. Some become trainers, coaches, managers, scouts, referees or umpires; radio or TV announcers; start their own business.

Average: major league baseball, $20,000; football, $26,000; basketball, hockey, $20,000 –$30,000. Some, $100,000 and more annually for a few years.

Very few opportunites, heavy competition.

OEK Brief No. 36
WORK Brief No. 259

OCCUPATION	PROGRAMMERS	PROJECTIONISTS, MOTION PICTURE
DUTIES	Write programs, or detailed coded instructions, for processing information with electronic computers. Determine data required and sequence of operations; write, code routines; make instruction sheets; test and debug programs.	Operate and maintain projector and sound equipment. Inspect film; load, start machine; adjust light and sound; make changeover to second machine at end of reel; rewind film. Splice film when required. May replace parts, make minor repairs; operate slide projector, spotlights.
WHERE EMPLOYED	Large business organizations such as banks, insurance companies, department stores; government agencies; industrial companies; universities and research laboratories; data-processing service centers.	Motion picture theaters and drive-ins throughout U.S. Some work for television stations and motion picture studios.
NUMBER OF WORKERS	Estimated 200,000, mostly men.	About 13,000; 5% women.
EDUCATION AND TRAINING	Most employers require college degree. About 1 year of on-the-job training.	High school diploma preferred. Most serve a 3-year apprenticeship.
SPECIAL QUALIFICATIONS	Numerical and spatial ability, reasoning ability, clarity of thought and expression, accuracy, ingenuity, reliability, patience.	Mechanical aptitude, manual dexterity, reliability, good eyesight and normal color vision, tolerance for routine work.
WAYS TO ENTER FIELD	Watch want ads in newspapers, listings in technical journals. Apply direct to organizations having computer system. Civil service offices list government openings.	Apply to union or direct to nonunion theaters, where a beginner may start as helper. A friend or relative who belongs to the union could be helpful.
CHANCE OF ADVANCEMENT	Good. Can become senior programmer, supervisor, systems analyst, executive or manager; start own service center.	Poor. Can switch to larger theater; in very large theater, become chief operator.
EARNINGS	Start: $8530 a year. Experienced: $12,200. Top: $20,000 or more.	Vary widely, depending on size and location of theater, hours. Range $2.95–$8.75 an hour.
SUPPLY AND DEMAND	One of the fastest-growing occupations; expect 35,000 openings a year throughout the 1970s. Women encouraged.	Number of projectionists decreasing. Much competition for few available openings.
REFERENCES	OEK Brief No. 281 WORK Brief No. 260	OEK Brief No. 279 WORK Brief No. 214

PROOFREADERS

Read proofs of type against original manuscript. With pencil, mark typographical errors, broken type, uneven spacing, improper indentation, type that does not conform to specifications, and uneven inking. May alternate with copyholder, reading manuscript copy aloud as proofreader follows proofs.

Printing and publishing companies that produce newspapers, magazines, books; commercial job printing and typesetting plants throughout U.S.

Undetermined number. A few more women than men.

High school graduation. Job printers and catalog publishers are the most willing to train on the job. Book publishers prefer proofreaders with some college education.

Good eyesight, accuracy, alertness, ability to work under pressure of deadlines. No objection to sedentary work. May have to pass test on grammar, spelling, punctuation, proofreaders' marks (found in many dictionaries).

Some start as copyholders. Apply direct to printing and publishing companies. Neighborhood job printer might be easiest place to gain experience. Check newspaper want ads, state and private employment services.

Somewhat limited. Proofreader may progress to editorial position if he has educational background and shows aptitude for editorial work.

Depend on experience, employer, and geographic area. Union journeymen: $5.15 an hour.

Not a large field, but almost indispensable in publishing and printing. Demand for trained people likely to remain fairly stable, with possibility of slight increase.

OEK Brief No. 373
WORK Brief No. 261

PSYCHIATRIC AIDES

Make beds, serve meals, feed and dress helpless patients, take patients on outings, talk with patients, and other work as assigned by supervisor.

In mental hospitals, psychiatric wards of general hospitals, mental health clinics.

Undetermined.

High school diploma useful, but not necessary. May have 1-week to 3-month on-the-job training.

Emotional maturity, interest in and liking for people, warm and understanding personality, patience, physical stamina.

Apply directly to hospital.

Limited. With experience and leadership ability, may advance to supervisory job.

Vary, depending on location and experience. In large cities, $120–$140 a week.

Severe shortage of mental health workers. Many jobs available for those with suitable personality and temperament.

WORK Brief No. 299

PSYCHIATRISTS

Use psychotherapy, electroconvulsive therapy, and drugs such as tranquilizers to prevent, diagnose, interpret, and treat mental and emotional illnesses. May teach, do research, write.

Most are in private practice. Others are on the staffs of hospitals, mental health clinics, medical schools, welfare and counseling agencies, research institutes. Mostly in large cities.

About 20,000; a small percentage women.

College degrees plus 4 years of medical school, 1-year internship, 5 years of residency and experience.

High level of intelligence, interest in people, empathy, integrity, emotional stability, patience, persistence. Must pass state exams to practice medicine, psychiatry.

May start as assistant to established psychiatrist, or may start own practice. Psychiatric journals, professional recommendations helpful.

Mostly by acquiring a reputation and expanding one's practice. Can become consultant, administrator.

Interns: $2000–$3000. Residents: $6000. In hospitals, clinics: $12,000–$28,000. In private practice: $20,000–$60,000 or more.

Dire shortage of psychiatrists; increasing demand. Some competition to enter medical school; after that, none.

OEK Brief No. 246
WORK Brief No. 264

OCCUPATION	PSYCHOLOGISTS	PUBLIC RELATIONS WORKERS
DUTIES	Study human behavior by means of psychological tests, personal interviews, case histories, experiments, surveys, and the like Usually specialize in one area of psychology. May teach, do research, advise and counsel clients.	Plan and prepare activities and communications to promote public opinion favorable to employer or client: write and edit articles, speeches, reports, pamphlets; do research; make contacts; arrange special events.
WHERE EMPLOYED	Most work in colleges and universities; others in government agencies, school systems, business and industry, research foundations and hospitals, consulting agencies. Some are self-employed.	Business and industrial companies; about 1500 public relations firms; trade, labor, and professional associations; colleges and universities; government agencies. Some are self-employed. Most work in sizable cities.
NUMBER OF WORKERS	About 40,000; 25% women.	About 75,000; 25% women.
EDUCATION AND TRAINING	Master's degree the minimum, Ph.D. required for most good positions. A year's internship usually required for clinical or counseling psychology.	College degree usually required. Suggested major: public relations, journalism, liberal arts, business.
SPECIAL QUALIFICATIONS	Scientific interests and aptitudes, high intelligence, liking for people, integrity, tact, patience, sympathy, good judgment. May need state license for private practice.	Writing ability, outgoing personality, imagination, drive, persuasive ability, initiative, fluency in conversation, persistence.
WAYS TO ENTER FIELD	University placement services; want ads in newspapers, notices in professional journals; civil service offices; direct application to employers.	Interview through college placement service, watch want ads, contact employment agencies, apply directly to employers. Many start as journalists, switch to public relations after gaining experience.
CHANCE OF ADVANCEMENT	Excellent for those with Ph.D. Can become professor, administrator, writer; start own practice or business.	Good for those with the right personal characteristics. Can become director, free-lance, start own agency.
EARNINGS	Start: $9000–$12,000. Experienced: $14,500–$16,300. Self-employed have highest incomes—up to $20,000 or more.	Start: $4600–$7500. Experienced: $9000–$13,000. Top: $25,000–$50,000.
SUPPLY AND DEMAND	Demand increasing more rapidly than supply in all areas of employment. Little competition for the 2800 openings annually.	Field growing rapidly, good chances for experienced people. Growing need for specialists. Over 4000 openings a year.
REFERENCES	OEK Brief No. 137 WORK Brief No. 68	OEK Brief No. 77 WORK Brief No. 267

PURCHASING AGENTS

Buy materials, equipment, supplies, and services. Contact suppliers, get bids or cost estimates, place orders, follow up to ensure prompt delivery. May meet with salesmen, visit suppliers' plants.

Manufacturing companies, wholesale and retail establishments, government agencies, hospitals, schools, other institutions—just about every sizable organization.

About 167,000 buyers and purchasing agents, not including store buyers; 9% women.

College degree desirable, required for most high-level positions. On-the-job training may last several weeks to a year.

Integrity, business sense, good judgment, dependability, responsibility, skill in human relations, eye for detail.

Without college degree, may start as clerk and become buyer only after much experience. With degree, may start as purchasing agent trainee, become junior buyer.

Fair. It may take years to become purchasing agent. From there, advancement is usually to top management jobs.

Start: $6300–$7500, with degree.

As industry expands and grows more complex, more purchasing agents will be needed. Expect 5400 openings yearly. Keen competition for top positions.

OEK Brief No. 97
WORK Brief No. 268

RANCHERS

Breed, raise, and market animals—beef cattle, sheep, hogs—for food; supervise farmhands; keep records. Watch over grazing cattle, feed hay and other rations, care for injured or sick animals, judge selling conditions, sell at auction or terminal market. May brand and dehorn animals, chase strays. May raise feed crops, inspect water, feed, and salt supplies.

Ranches in the Great Plains, South and Southwest, intermountain regions of the West; farms and feedlots in the Midwest; other rural areas.

Number uncertain. Some women, particularly as owners.

Cowhands, no educational requirements to meet. Owners and managers find college training in agriculture and animal husbandry an advantage. Future Farmers or 4-H cattle projects are excellent training.

Enjoy working outdoors, with animals. Rancher needs physical strength, endurance. Owners and managers need knowledge of scientific breeding and feeding, business acumen.

Those who are born and bred on farm or ranch often go into this work. Others start as farm laborers or cowhands. Get job leads from state employment service, farm organizations in desired area.

Manage feedlot or ranch. Buy one's own land and foundation herd—but this takes a lot of capital. Once the rancher has his own business, he can enlarge it gradually.

Vary widely from year to year. 1970 figures: Cattle ranchers in Southwest, $10,000; in Northwest, $25,000. Sheep ranchers, $20,000. Shepherds, $4000. Cowhands, $3600.

Long-range outlook is quite good, as beef consumption increases. Capital outlay and economic risks involved make large operation almost essential, cutting down on number of small ranches and farms.

OEK Brief No. 42
WORK Brief No. 272

REAL ESTATE AGENTS AND BROKERS

Sell, buy, rent, and manage land, houses, and commercial buildings. Brokers advertise properties, handle financing and legal details, manage business. Agents call on clients, show properties, negotiate, make sales.

Throughout U.S., especially in and around urban areas. Most brokers are independent businessmen. Agents work for brokers, banks, insurance companies, large real estate companies.

More than 226,000 real estate agents and brokers: ⅓ women. About 500,000 more are part-time salespeople.

High school required, some college training preferred. Some experience needed to become broker in most states.

Must pass exam for state license. Sales ability, knowledge of community, liking for people, courtesy, tact, neat appearance, patience.

Can start as a part-time agent or assistant in a real estate office. Check with local real estate board, apply to broker or other employer.

Mostly in terms of increasing earnings. An agent can become manager, go into business for himself as a broker.

Usually paid a straight commission. Experienced agents: $7000–$12,000 a year. Brokers: to $20,000 or more.

About 15,000 openings a year. Jobs are easy to get, but competition for sales is keen, especially during times of slow economic activity.

OEK Brief No. 169
WORK Brief No. 274

OCCUPATION	REAL ESTATE APPRAISERS	RECEPTIONISTS AND SWITCHBOARD OPERATORS
DUTIES	Estimate market value of land, buildings for legal, financial, tax, business purposes. Study location, physical condition, equipment, cost of upkeep, depreciation; check records; photograph or sketch property; write detailed report.	Usually stationed near entrance to building or office. Greet visitors, obtain names and purposes, give information and directions. Operate PBX switchboard. May do typing, record keeping, other work.
WHERE EMPLOYED	Local, state, and federal government agencies; real estate companies, including some that specialize in appraisal; insurance companies, banks, other financial institutions. Some work as consultants.	Almost all large and medium-sized offices, businesses, industrial plants, hospitals, public buildings have jobs for receptionists and switchboard operators.
NUMBER OF WORKERS	Estimated 55,000; some women.	About 298,000 receptionists, 168,000 switchboard operators; less than 5% men.
EDUCATION AND TRAINING	College degree usually required, plus real estate experience. Some large companies have training programs.	High school graduation preferred. Business courses are assets. A few days of on-the-job training usually given.
SPECIAL QUALIFICATIONS	Knowledge of real estate, economics; business ability, thoroughness, attention to detail, honesty, responsibility, tact, sound judgment.	Manual dexterity, neat and attractive appearance, pleasant voice, tact, courtesy, good memory, poise, even temper.
WAYS TO ENTER FIELD	Previous experience as real estate agent, broker, or building contractor is usually necessary. After getting experience, apply to employers or civil service office.	Watch newspaper want ads, listings of employment agencies and civil service offices. Apply direct to organization employing receptionists.
CHANCE OF ADVANCEMENT	Can become chief appraiser, start own appraising business.	Limited. Can move to better job with same company, but some will require more education.
EARNINGS	Trainees: $550–$800 a month. Experienced: $800–$1200 a month. Top: $30,000–$50,000 a year.	In industry: $5109–$6010. In government: $4621–$6778.
SUPPLY AND DEMAND	Outlook very good. Growing demand for appraisers expected to continue. Considerable competition for positions at all levels.	Many openings owing to growth of business and high turnover rate. Competition may be keen for 24,000 receptionist openings annually.
REFERENCES	OEK Brief No. 364 WORK Brief No. 275	OEK Brief Nos. 278, 356 WORK Brief Nos. 276, 315

RECREATION WORKERS

Help people enjoy and use leisure time constructively by organizing individual and group activities and by administering physical, social, and cultural programs for all age groups. May operate recreational facilities and study recreation needs of individuals and communities.

With government agencies; with organizations such as the YMCA, YWCA, and the Red Cross; with hospitals, children's homes, boys clubs; with industrial and business organizations.

About 13,500 full-time workers. Many thousands more work part time.

A college degree is required for almost all supervisory jobs. May major in recreation, social science, or physical education.

Good health, emotional maturity, warm personality, leadership ability.

Through personal contacts made while working part time after school or in the summer. Also by direct application to an agency that hires recreation workers.

Good. Beginners can advance to playground leader, camp director, recreation director. May also go into related fields, such as social work or physical education.

Start: $7200–$7800. Experienced: $8500–$10,000. Top: to $22,000.

Great demand for competent workers. Expect at least 1700 openings a year throughout the 1970s.

OEK Brief No. 78
WORK Brief No. 277

REPAIRMEN, AUTOMOBILE BODY

Repair damaged auto bodies, fenders, and frames. Hammer, weld, file, solder metal. May paint body, replace parts, give cost estimates. Use hammers, spoons, dolly blocks, wrenches, jacks, files, and many other tools.

Service departments of automobile dealers; body repair shops and garages; garages of cab, bus, and truck companies; auto manufacturing plants. Throughout U.S., but most work in cities.

About 100,000 men.

High school diploma preferred. Shop courses or trade school helpful. 4-year apprenticeship available in some areas.

Mechanical ability, physical strength and stamina, skill with hand and power tools, pride in workmanship, tolerance for noise and dirt.

Unions, want ads, state employment service, direct application. May start as helper or apprentice.

Poor in small repair shops. Those who work for dealers can become foreman or service manager. Can open own shop.

Journeymen: average, $3.60 an hour. Beginners: less than half as much. May be paid on incentive system. Top: $9000–$18,000 a year.

Shortage of trained body repairmen, but employers want dependable workmen to fill 4500 openings each year.

OEK Brief No. 301
WORK Brief No. 31

REPAIRMEN, INSTRUMENT

Install, maintain, repair instruments used to measure, record, or control electricity, heat, pressure, flow of liquids, time, or other variables. Use test equipment to locate source of trouble, hand tools to repair. Specialize in one kind of instrument.

Instrument manufacturing concerns, companies that use instruments in manufacturing or processing, public utilities, airlines, and government agencies. Most work in cities.

More than 95,000, almost all men.

High school diploma. Technical institute training an advantage. On-the-job training may last several weeks to 4 years. Apprenticeships available in some locations.

Mechanical aptitude, manual dexterity, spatial perception; knowledge of math, electricity, electronics; persistence, ability to work alone.

Placement bureaus of technical schools; want ads in newspapers, technical magazines; application to state employment agencies, unions, employers.

Excellent. Can become foreman, service representative, technician, troubleshooter, engineering assistant.

$2.93–$4.77 an hour.

Increase expected as demand for instruments grows, but training requirements will become tougher. Estimate 6000 openings a year.

OEK Brief No. 334
WORK Brief No. 168

OCCUPATION	REPAIRMEN, SHOE	REPAIRMEN, WATCH
DUTIES	Repair, rebuild, dye. polish, stretch shoes. Replace worn-out heels and soles, repair torn or scuffed uppers. May sell shoe polish, laces, other accessories; repair handbags, other leather items. Use machine and hand tools.	Clean, oil, repair, test, and adjust watches and other timepieces. Disassemble, locate source of trouble, repair or replace defective parts, clean and adjust. Use small hand tools, machine tools, and test instruments.
WHERE EMPLOYED	In shoe repair shops, and in combination shoe repair, laundry, and drycleaning establishments throughout U.S.	Watch repair shops, jewelry shops (both wholesale and retail), department stores, watch manufacturing companies.
NUMBER OF WORKERS	About 25,000; 4% women.	About 15,000, mostly men.
EDUCATION AND TRAINING	Learn the work in vocational or trade school, 1–3 years apprenticeship, or on-the-job training.	High school preferred, plus 1 or 2 years of trade school or 2–4 years of on-the-job training.
SPECIAL QUALIFICATIONS	Mechanical ability, manual dexterity, steady hands, good eyesight, courtesy, friendliness, ability to work steadily. Owners need managerial, business abilities.	Good eyesight, steady hand, patience, finger dexterity, mechanical aptitude, ability to concentrate. Friendliness, tact for shopowners. May need state license.
WAYS TO ENTER FIELD	Apply to shoe repair shops. Watch want ads in newspapers. Visit state employment office. Trade school placement service may help.	Placement service of watchmaking school, newspaper want ads, state employment service, direct application to employers.
CHANCE OF ADVANCEMENT	After getting experience, good chance to open own shop or buy an established one.	Good chance to start own business, become instrument maker or repairman.
EARNINGS	Start: $64 a week. Skilled men: $96–$120 a week. Owners: $5000–$15,000 a year.	Start: $90–$125 a week. Skilled repairmen: $200 or more a week.
SUPPLY AND DEMAND	Newcomers needed, but few apprenticeships available. Skilled workers in demand for 1000 openings a year.	Extreme shortage of trained people. Beginners needed to work especially on miniature devices such as transistors.
REFERENCES	OEK Brief No. 157 WORK Brief No. 296	OEK Brief No. 179 WORK Brief No. 337

REPORTERS

Collect information, take notes, write or phone in news stories. May cover beat, interview newsworthy persons, cover special events. May specialize in one area of news. On small papers, may take photographs, do editorial work.

Newspapers, newsmagazines, wire-service bureaus, radio and TV stations and networks, trade publications, house organs, public relations firms, government agencies.

About 39,000 men and women.

College degree in journalism or liberal arts. Broad background in any form of communications.

Good background of knowledge, writing skill, persistence, resourcefulness, good memory, accuracy, curiosity, physical stamina. Skill in typing helps.

Apply to personnel office of newspaper or other employer. Most start on small papers or magazines. College placement office can be helpful in locating first job.

Good chance to switch to better position, become editor, correspondent. Some become columnists, news analysts.

Cub reporters: $150–$185 a week. Experienced: $200–$300 or more a week. Top salaries in TV, newsmagazines.

Competition strong, but outlook good. Expect about 1650 openings a year throughout the 1970s.

OEK Brief No. 216
WORK Brief No. 280

ROOFERS

Install, alter, repair roofing, using such materials as sheet metal, tile, slate, asphalt shingles, composition, felt, tar, and gravel. Cut materials, nail to base; may spread tar and gravel to weatherproof surface. May waterproof walls, tanks.

Roofing and general contracting firms, government agencies, large industrial concerns.

About 60,000, almost all men.

High school desirable, plus 3-year apprenticeship or longer period of on-the-job training.

Good physical condition, agility, manual dexterity, basic knowledge of arithmetic; preference for outdoor work. Fear of heights will disqualify an applicant.

Apply to roofing contractor, union office, or local apprenticeship committee

Fair. Can become foreman, superintendent, free-lance roofer, roofing contractor.

Journeymen: union minimum for composition roofers, $6.95; for slate and tile roofers, $6.70. Apprentices start at 65% of journeyman wage.

Demand depends on amount of construction, but estimate 3000 openings a year. Some increase in numbers of roofers expected.

OEK Brief No. 299
WORK Brief No. 282

ROUTEMEN

Drive light trucks over a set route, selling and delivering goods or providing services to customers in homes or shops. Load trucks, deliver goods and make pickups, collect money, take orders, keep records, try to acquire new customers.

Wholesale and retail firms that provide a wide variety of goods and services, such as dairies, bakeries, beverage distributors, drycleaning plants, laundries and diaper services, newspapers. Most work in or near large cities.

About 242,000 deliverymen and routemen; 3% women.

High school diploma desirable, sometimes required. A few weeks of on-the-job training usually given.

Pleasant personality, sales ability, driving skill, stamina, neat appearance, knowledge of basic arithmetic, reliability, tact. Need chauffeur's license in most states.

Watch want ads in newspapers. Apply to state employment agency or direct to employers. May start as helper.

May obtain better route, become foreman or supervisor, move from retail to wholesale, which usually pays more. Become salesman.

Most are paid salary plus commission. Start: retail routemen, $100–$150 a week; wholesale, $130–$240.

Demand increasing in some industries, declining in others. About 2600 openings a year; fair amount of competition.

WORK Brief No. 283

OCCUPATION	ROUTEMEN, AUTOMATIC VENDING	SALESMEN, AUTOMOBILE
DUTIES	Install automatic vending machines; clean machines and make adjustments and minor repairs; remove stale. outdated, or damaged merchandise; fill machines with fresh stock; keep sales records on individual items; remove money. Load and unload delivery truck with stock. May seek new machine locations, analyze customer preferences.	Sell new and used automobiles and trucks. Contact prospects, appraise trade-in value of old car, arrange for financing, servicing, and delivery of new car.
WHERE EMPLOYED	In about 6200 automatic vending companies throughout U.S., mostly in large cities. About 1400 routemen operate their own one-man business.	Work for new-car dealers and many thousands of used-car dealers throughout U.S.
NUMBER OF WORKERS	20,000 men.	Estimated 120,000; very few women.
EDUCATION AND TRAINING	Most beginners are high school graduates. Start as trainees, watching and helping experienced men. Some employers provide formal training for a few days to a year before men are assigned a regular route.	High school diploma usually required. Some college preferred. Some dealers and car manufacturers have formal training programs.
SPECIAL QUALIFICATIONS	Neat appearance, friendliness, courtesy, tact, mechanical aptitude, average or better physical condition and stamina, liking for active work. Must have state driver's license.	Sales ability, tact, self-confidence, pleasing personality. Must be able to think quickly, calculate rapidly, and express oneself well in conversation. Need license in some states.
WAYS TO ENTER FIELD	Newspaper want ads, employment agencies provide leads. Apply direct to vending companies.	Apply direct to dealer or agency. Personal contacts helpful in getting first job. Want ads sometimes list openings for auto salesmen.
CHANCE OF ADVANCEMENT	May become resident serviceman, caring for many machines in one location; route supervisor; or branch manager. Some shift to machine mechanic and may advance to senior mechanic, shop foreman, or supervisor.	Limited; mostly in terms of a chance to earn more in commissions. Some experienced men open their own dealerships.
EARNINGS	Majority of workers earn $2.75–$4 an hour. Some make more.	Most are paid commission or salary plus commission. Average: $143–$234 a week. May reach $20,000 or more a year. Top salesman in country: $100,000.
SUPPLY AND DEMAND	Expect business to increase at the rate of 7%–9% annually, creating many opportunities for employment in this field. Trend is toward larger companies rather than one-man operations.	Expect increase in number of men, but demand depends on economic conditions. Those with proven ability to sell cars can always get one of the 4300 jobs open each year.
REFERENCES	OEK Brief No. 122 WORK Brief No. 30	OEK Brief No. 111 WORK Brief No. 33

SALESMEN, MANUFACTURERS'

Call on officials of wholesale firms, large retail stores, industrial companies, institutions, to promote and sell a product or line of products. Demonstrate samples, take orders, arrange delivery. May collect payment, plan work, keep records.

Home or branch offices of manufacturers. Manufacturers' agents, or representatives, have their own separate offices.

About 500,000; 10% women, mostly in food products industries.

At least high school. College degree in business or engineering usually preferred. On-the-job training given, sometimes a year or more

Sales ability, friendliness, neat appearance, interest in people, drive, persistence, understanding of human nature.

On-campus interviews, school placement services, newspaper and technical journal want ads. Direct application to manufacturing companies.

Can increase income as selling ability or knowledge increases. Can advance to sales manager, executive; start own business.

Usually paid salary plus commission. Beginners: $8500 a year. Experienced: $16,000–$22,000 or more.

Demand increasing, but so are requirements. Topflight salesmen with college or technical education will be most in demand for the 25,000 job openings expected each year.

OEK Brief No. 114
WORK Brief No. 197

SALESMEN, RADIO-TV TIME

Sell radio and TV broadcasting time to sponsors, advertising agencies, other clients. Visit clients, explain station's programs, coverage rates; try to sell programs or spot announcements. May help plan advertising.

At 5600 radio and 700 TV broadcasting stations. Throughout U.S. in cities over 10,000.

About 20 000; a few women, mostly in small stations.

College training highly recommended. Some on-the-job training given.

Sales ability, intelligence. broad range of knowledge and interests, imagination, attractive appearance and personality, liking for people, ambition, initiative.

Apply to sales managers of stations. Experience in broadcasting, sales, advertising, or journalism usually required to start as a time salesman.

Mostly in terms of increasing earnings. May switch to larger station; become sales manager.

Usually get 10%–25% commission plus small salary. Top: $15,000 or more.

Expect increase in number of salesmen. About 10,000 openings a year. Keen competition for openings, sales.

OEK Brief No. 347
WORK Brief No. 271

SALESPEOPLE, HOUSE-TO-HOUSE

Call on prospective customers in their homes, demonstrate or display products or explain services, take orders, collect deposit or payment. Keep records and accounts, make prospect lists, plan sales campaigns, arrange for deliveries.

With companies that sell goods and services house to house. In large and small communities throughout U.S.

About 2 million, many of whom work part time; 50% women.

No definite requirements. High school and college helpful. May get several days on-the-job training with experienced salesperson.

Sales ability, sincerity, attractive appearance, self-confidence, poise, perseverance, knowledge of motivation, good speaking voice. Physical stamina may be necessary.

Watch want ads in newspapers and magazines. Apply direct to companies that use this sales system.

Mostly in terms of improving technique, increasing earnings. Can become manager or executive of direct-selling company.

Usually work on straight 10%–40% commission. Average for full-time salespeople: $6000–$7000. Many earn $10,000; some more.

Direct-selling companies always have openings to fill, and almost any presentable applicant will get a tryout.

OEK Brief No. 237
WORK Brief No. 159

OCCUPATION	SALESPEOPLE, RETAIL STORE	SANITARIANS, PUBLIC HEALTH
DUTIES	Determine customer's needs and preferences, show merchandise, answer questions, sell. Take payment and make change, fill out charge or sales slip, wrap purchases. May check and order stock, handle exchanges, keep merchandise neatly arranged.	Apply technical knowledge to environmental health. Inspect recreation facilities, food and dairy plants, restaurants, waste-disposal facilities, water-supply systems, public housing to ensure compliance with health regulations. Plan, supervise public health programs.
WHERE EMPLOYED	Retail stores of all kinds and sizes throughout U.S. Department stores employ largest numbers.	Federal, state. and local government agencies. Mostly in heavily populated cities and towns throughout U.S. Some work for U.S. agencies in South America, Asia, Africa.
NUMBER OF WORKERS	About 2.5 million; 60% women.	15,000.
EDUCATION AND TRAINING	High school graduates preferred in most stores. A few days of on-the-job training usually given.	College degree required. Graduate degree needed for advancement to responsible positions.
SPECIAL QUALIFICATIONS	Sales ability, knowledge of product, pleasant personality, liking for people, physical stamina, neat appearance, courtesy, tact.	Aptitude for science; tact, persuasive ability, liking for people, perseverance. integrity. In many states must be licensed.
WAYS TO ENTER FIELD	High school distributive education program helpful, as is a part-time or summer job in a retail store. Apply to personnel office of store.	Apply to health department, civil service office. Watch notices in professional journals. Usually start as junior sanitarian.
CHANCE OF ADVANCEMENT	Limited in small stores. In department store, can become buyer, manager; move to department or store where earnings are greater.	To senior sanitarian, supervisor, field supervisor, administrator. Ph.D. preferred for top positions.
EARNINGS	Start: $1.60 or more an hour. Experienced people may get $3 or more an hour. Some stores pay salary plus commission.	Start: $7000–$7500 a year. Experienced: $10,000–$14,000. Top: to $30,000.
SUPPLY AND DEMAND	High turnover creates many job openings. Occupation is expected to increase somewhat in size. About 130,000 openings a year.	About 1100 job openings each year. Experienced sanitarians are in great demand. Average competition for advancement.
REFERENCES	OEK Brief No. 239 WORK Brief Nos. 90, 100, 311	OEK Brief No. 248 WORK Brief No. 287

SCIENTISTS, CROP AND SOIL

Apply scientific knowledge and methods to crop production and soil management. Study and classify soils and crops; develop new breeds, fertilizers, conservation practices. May do research, teach, advise farmers, manage farms.

Federal and state government agencies; colleges and universities; companies that process, manufacture, buy, market agricultural products and equipment; financial and real estate firms. Some are consultants.

About 15,000; 5% women especially in research.

Bachelor's degree in agronomy the minimum. Graduate degree essential for teaching, research, better jobs.

Interest in science, scientific aptitude, analytical ability, curiosity, perseverance, accuracy. Must take exam for government positions.

Can start in government work through summer training programs while still in college. College placement services, listings in technical journals, direct application.

Excellent. Can become research director, manager, professor, administrator, consultant.

Start: $600–$700 a month. Experienced: $10,000–$17,000. Top: $20,000 or more.

Demand growing for those with graduate degrees, especially in soil science.

OEK Brief Nos. 22, 211
WORK Brief No. 81

SECRETARIES

Take notes and dictation, transcribe, type letters and reports; greet callers, answer telephone; schedule appointments, meetings, trips; read and sort mail; file; keep records. May specialize as legal or medical secretary, shorthand reporter.

Every kind of business, industry, government agency, and nonprofit organization.

About 2.8 million secretaries and stenographers; less than 5% men.

At least high school. Training in business school, junior college, or college helpful.

Friendly personality, liking for people, tact, discretion, dependability, accuracy, courtesy, good memory, neat appearance. Knowledge of grammar, spelling.

Watch want ads, civil service announcements. Employment agencies and school placement services helpful. Direct application to employers. May start as clerk typist, stenographer.

Limited. Some become executive secretaries, administrative assistants, department heads.

Range: in industry, $6259–$8147; in government, $5853–$10,528. Executive secretaries and those with supervisory experience earn more.

Demand far exceeds supply. Many openings because of turnover. Little competition for experienced secretaries. Demand for men.

OEK Brief Nos. 19, 300
WORK Brief No. 288

SECURITIES SALESMEN

For individual and corporate customers, buy and sell orders for stocks, bonds, shares in mutual funds. May offer suggestions to customer about purchase or sale of particular securities, furnish information about certain types of investments, provide latest stock quotations and information about activities and financial positions of corporations.

Main and branch offices of securities or brokerage firms, investment bankers, mutual fund firms throughout U.S. Most cities of 50,000 or more population have one or more such offices.

200,000 men and women. About 60% are full-time salesmen for securities firms; 40% part-time for mutual funds.

College training preferred; degree in business administration, economics, liberal arts. Most employers provide training for beginners; program often lasts six months or longer.

Absolute trustworthiness and responsibility, alertness, attention to detail, tact. Most states require licensing. Securities exchanges require registration, for which salesmen must pass written exam.

Direct application to brokerage offices, investment bankers, mutual fund firms. Most beginners start on some other job than selling.

Salesman is most sought-after job in brokerage houses. Some salesmen become partners or officers; usually they continue to serve a few select customers.

Income depends on ability. Sales trainee earns about $650 a month. After five years, average $10,000; may make up to $20,000. Top management: $25,000 and up.

Employment expected to rise gradually. Turnover high among beginners. About 12,000 openings a year throughout the 1970s. Capable women encouraged.

OEK Brief No. 165
WORK Brief No. 287

OCCUPATION	SERVICE REPRESENTATIVES FOR PUBLIC UTILITIES	SERVICE STATION ATTENDANTS
DUTIES	Accept orders for service to be installed, turned on, changed, temporarily shut off, discontinued; explain advantages and costs of various types of service; receive information about service malfunctions, dispatch repair crew. May explain company regulations, answer questions relating to service. Customer contacts may be primarily by telephone.	Fill gas and oil tanks, check water and tires, clean windshields; perform automobile maintenance work and make minor repairs; sell and install tires, batteries, other parts and accessories; take payment and make change; keep records.
WHERE EMPLOYED	Telephone, gas, electric light and power companies throughout U.S.	Gasoline service stations, and service garages of government agencies, transportation companies, and large industrial organizations.
NUMBER OF WORKERS	Variable. Majority are women.	About 410,000 service station attendants; a few women.
EDUCATION AND TRAINING	High school diploma; business training or typing skill usually valuable. College education helpful for advancement. On-the-job training usually ranges from 2 to 7 weeks.	No special education requirements, but high school preferred. Formal and on-the-job training may last 2–8 weeks.
SPECIAL QUALIFICATIONS	Pleasant telephone voice and manner, tact, good judgment, initiative, responsibility, alertness, ability to express oneself clearly. Municipally owned utilities usually require civil service test.	Manual dexterity, mechanical aptitude, physical stamina, neat appearance, tact, courtesy, alertness. Sales ability, reliability, pleasing personality are desirable.
WAYS TO ENTER FIELD	Apply direct to utility company. Telephone companies place beginners directly in service representative jobs; gas and electric companies usually start them in another job. Watch newspaper want ads; check state and private employment services and city civil service commission.	Apply direct to service stations, watch want ads, visit state employment service office.
CHANCE OF ADVANCEMENT	Some start in clerical work, advance to service representative. May advance to representative-trainee instructor, supervisor, neighborhood office supervisor, personnel or staff assistant. Some shift to larger company.	Limited. With training and experience, can become mechanic, station manager, owner.
EARNINGS	Start: telephone companies, $110 a week; gas and electric, $187–$209.	$1.80–$2.91 an hour. May receive commission on sales.
SUPPLY AND DEMAND	Some competition for jobs. Utilities always on the lookout for capable people to do work that can never be done by machine.	Large occupation with high turnover, about 13,000 openings annually. Sizable increase expected in jobs in next ten years.
REFERENCES	OEK Brief No. 372 WORK Brief No. 290	OEK Brief No. 60 WORK Brief No. 291

SERVICEMEN, ELECTRONIC DATA-PROCESSING MACHINE

Install, maintain, and repair electronic computers and related data-processing machines. Adjust, clean, disassemble; check circuits; diagnose and locate cause of trouble; replace defective parts. Use hand tools, testing instruments.

Most work for manufacturers of data-processing equipment. Others work for government agencies, industrial firms, banks and insurance companies, public utilities, data-processing centers.

More than 30,000 men.

High school and several months of company schooling, plus on-the-job training.

Aptitude for math, mechanics. Analytical ability, persistence, accuracy, ability to work under pressure reliability. Neat appearance, likable manner helpful.

Placement service of technical school may be helpful. Apply direct to manufacturer or other employer. See newspaper want ads, state employment service.

Good chance to become supervisor, technical assistant, service manager. May switch to sales or production work.

Start: about $105 a week. Experienced: about $300 a week.

One of the fastest-growing job fields. Shortage of qualified men. Some competition for entry positions.

OEK Brief No. 323
WORK Brief No. 108

SERVICEMEN, HOME APPLIANCE

Install, maintain, and repair electrical and gas-burning home appliances, such as refrigerators, ranges, laundry equipment. furnaces. Find cause of trouble; clean, repair, or replace defective parts. May drive truck, make home calls; give estimates, advice.

Appliance stores, department stores, repair shops, gas and electric companies, manufacturers and wholesalers of home appliances.

About 205,000 men.

High school plus up to 3 years of on-the-job training and experience. Technical or trade school training helpful.

Mechanical ability, manual dexterity, good eyesight, friendliness, tact, courtesy, neat appearance. problem-solving ability.

Apply direct to employer, watch want ads in newspapers, visit state employment agency. May start as helper, trainee.

Good. Can become foreman, service manager, salesman, instructor; start own repair shop.

$2.18–$4.22 an hour. Self-employed workers may earn more.

Growing occupation; demand far outweighs supply of trained workers. Considerable competition for best jobs.

OEK Brief No. 333
WORK Brief No. 152

SERVICEMEN, OFFICE MACHINE

Clean, adjust, service, repair, maintain typewriters and adding, mailing, calculating, accounting-bookkeeping, and dictating machines. Usually specialize in one kind or make of machine.

About half work in the service departments of manufacturers; another large number for independent repair, sales, service shops; the rest for large organizations or government agencies.

About 74,000, almost all men.

High school diploma usually required. Some attend company schools for 1–10 weeks. On-the-job training may last 1–3 years.

Mechanical aptitude, manual dexterity, tact. Should be responsible, able to work without supervision.

Apply direct to office machine manufacturer, service firm, or civil service office. Visit state employment agency to learn of openings; read want ads.

Can become supervisor, service manager, training instructor; enter sales or executive position; start own repair business.

Experienced: $8000–$13,000 a year. Those who service more complex machines earn most.

Demand increasing. Expect 6000 openings a year throughout the 1970s. Competition fairly heavy.

OEK Brief No. 154
WORK Brief No. 224

OCCUPATION	SERVICEMEN, RADIO-TV	SEWING MACHINE OPERATORS
DUTIES	Install, service, and repair radios, TV sets, phonographs, hi-fis, and the like; may specialize in one. Locate cause of trouble, replace or repair malfunctioning parts. May make home service calls, do shopwork. Use hand tools, testing equipment.	Operate power sewing machines; stitch together parts of garments, curtains, drapes, upholstery, other items made from cloth, plastic, leather. May specialize in one operation or do all sewing work needed to produce a garment.
WHERE EMPLOYED	Independent repair shops, service departments of large stores and radio-TV dealers, manufacturers and wholesalers of electronic equipment, government agencies.	Most work in garment factories, especially in New York and other big cities; some for companies that make curtains and draperies, plastic and leather products, upholstered furniture, auto seatcovers, canvas products, caskets.
NUMBER OF WORKERS	About 132,000; less than 2% women.	About 600,000; 6% men.
EDUCATION AND TRAINING	High school plus 2 or 3 years training in trade or technical school and on the job.	No specific requirements. On-the-job training may take a week to several months.
SPECIAL QUALIFICATIONS	Aptitude for electronics, mechanical ability, manual dexterity, good eyesight, reliability, tact, courtesy. Business ability for shop-owners, managers. Some states, cities require license.	Finger dexterity, good coordination, good eyesight; ability to concentrate , work steadily and rapidly, follow instructions; tolerance of routine.
WAYS TO ENTER FIELD	Watch want ads, inquire at placement bureau of trade or technical school, apply direct to employers, visit state employment agency.	Apply to garment factories. Union offices and state employment service may have information about factories that are hiring.
CHANCE OF ADVANCEMENT	Good chance to become foreman, manager, technician; or can open own shop.	Mostly in terms of increasing earnings by improving proficiency. Can become foreman or forelady.
EARNINGS	Start: $85–$100 a week. Experienced: $125–$160 or more. Managers and owners make more.	Earnings depend on speed, skill, type of garment, and location. Nationwide average, men's suits and coats: $2.77. Women's: $3.64–$4.89 in New York area.
SUPPLY AND DEMAND	Demand rapidly increasing. Best chances for men with broad and up-to-date electronics training. Expect 4500 openings a year throughout the 1970s.	Occupation expected to expand slowly; many openings because of high rate of turnover. Experienced operators in demand.
REFERENCES	OEK Brief No. 346 WORK Brief No. 270	OEK Brief No. 351 WORK Brief No. 292

SHEET METAL WORKERS	SHIP PILOTS	SHORTHAND REPORTERS
Make, install, and repair sheet metal products such as ventilating, air-conditioning, and heating ducts, roofing, siding, rainspouts. Lay out work, cut and shape metal, assemble, install. Use hand and machine tools.	Responsible for guiding ships safely into ports. Read navigation charts, use radar equipment, direct wheelsman on prescribed course.	Record proceedings, usually word for word, by machine or in written shorthand in law courts, legislative hearings, United Nations sessions, business and professional conventions, press conferences, meetings of boards of directors, stockholders, and others. Transcribe notes, or dictate them onto tapes or records, which are transcribed by typists.
Manufacturing plants that produce sheet-metal equipment, heating and air-conditioning contractors, roofing contractors, government agencies, shipyards, aircraft builders, railroads. Some are self-employed.	In ocean ports, most lake ports, some river ports.	Courts of all types throughout U.S ; Congress and state legislatures in capital cities; United Nations in New York; reporting agencies; or as self-employed reporter, usually in large cities.
About 60,000 men.	Undetermined. 1000 in American Pilots' Association.	About 9000; estimated 60% men and 40% women. Majority are court reporters.
High school preferred, plus 4-year apprenticeship. Some learn through on-the-job training.	High school graduation necessary, then years of special training and shipboard experience. Training at special academy that prepares merchant marine officers highly recommended.	High school graduation; some college desirable. Specific training, usually business or secretarial school, to enable reporter to take dictation at 200 words a minute; also training in transcribing.
Manual dexterity, mechanical aptitude, physical stamina, agility, accuracy, spatial perception.	Outdoor and scientific interest, manual dexterity, good judgment, stamina. Must pass difficult Coast Guard exam for license	Good knowledge of medical terminology, legal and Latin words and phrases. business law, English grammar and punctuation. Good vocabulary, unimpaired hearing, alertness. Government jobs usually require passing civil service examination.
Apply to union office. contractors, and manufacturing plants. Visit state employment agency. Watch want ads. May start as helper.	Will be assigned to ship at the end of a formal training program. Without formal training, apply for work at a central hiring hall in one of the chief ports in the country.	Secretarial and business colleges and National Shorthand Reporters Assn. provide placement service. Apply to reporting agencies, check state employment service and U.S. and state civil service commissions, watch newspaper ads.
Fair. Can become foreman, superintendent, contractor.	Pilot is a top job. It takes at least nine years to work up from third mate.	Limited. Some establish their own reporting business, perhaps employing other reporters.
In building construction: average $7.64 an hour. Apprentices start at 50% of journeyman rates.	Start: about $12,000. Experienced: $25,000 or more. Top: $30,000 or more.	$4000–$13,000 a year for court reporters and federal employees. Others, depending on assignments, reputation, and number of clients, may make up to $375 a week.
Skilled men in demand. Gradual increase in employment expected, especially in construction of air-conditioning ducts. Over 2500 openings each year.	Jobs declining; competition very keen.	Considerable shortage of and increasing demand for capable shorthand reporters.
OEK Brief No. 89 WORK Brief No. 293	WORK Brief No. 294	OEK Brief No. 93 WORK Brief No. 297

OCCUPATION	SINGERS	SOCIAL WORKERS
DUTIES	Give vocal performances as soloists or in groups; make recordings; appear in films, on radio, TV, stage. May give private voice lessons, teach, direct choirs.	Attempt to alleviate or solve social problems; give advice; arrange for medical, rehabilitative, financial assistance; refer clients to counseling and homemaking services, foster homes, housing facilities. May plan and direct group activities.
WHERE EMPLOYED	Choirs, opera, concert performances, motion pictures, TV, radio, nightclubs and supper clubs, conventions and industrial shows, schools, music conservatories, churches, synagogues. Throughout U.S., mostly in large cities.	Public and private welfare agencies, hospitals and clinics, schools and colleges, community centers and settlement houses, other social agencies and institutions. Most work in urban areas.
NUMBER OF WORKERS	About 75,000 professional singers and singing teachers, men and women.	About 170,000; 40% men.
EDUCATION AND TRAINING	Start piano lessons at early age, formal voice training in early teens, continue 3–10 years. Popular singers, little or no training. High school diploma recommended; college required for teaching.	College degree is the minimum. Graduate degree in social work required for certification, leading to better starting jobs and advancement.
SPECIAL QUALIFICATIONS	Above-average singing voice, outstanding personality, attractive appearance, physical stamina, some dancing and acting ability, perseverance, good contacts, and luck. Other skill or ability to support oneself when singing jobs are few.	Interest in and liking for people, sympathy, tolerance. emotional maturity, perseverance, resourcefulness, good judgment, impartiality. Leadership qualities important.
WAYS TO ENTER FIELD	Voice teacher can help arrange auditions; work through booking agency; apply to local theater, band or combo, choral groups, churches, music festivals. Send tape or record to radio station managers, record producers, or try for personal auditions.	College placement services helpful. Apply to civil service offices or direct to welfare agencies, other employers.
CHANCE OF ADVANCEMENT	Limited. Those with talent and persistence may progress from choral to solo work, or from local to national (and possibly international) acceptance and acclaim.	Good for those with graduate degree. Can become specialist, supervisor, administrator, teacher, research worker.
EARNINGS	Vary greatly. Teachers' salaries depend on school system or economic status of community. Performers usually supplement their incomes by doing other work.	Start: $9000–$10,500 a year. Experienced: $15,000–$20,000. Top: $45,000.
SUPPLY AND DEMAND	Intense competition, especially among popular singers; little growth in employment opportunities. Ample employment for elementary, high school, college teachers.	Acute shortage of social workers; men with graduate degrees in particular demand. Little competition. About 18,000 openings a year.
REFERENCES	OEK Brief No. 309 WORK Brief No. 298	OEK Brief No. 80 WORK Brief Nos. 299, 300

SOCIAL WORKERS, PSYCHIATRIC	SOCIOLOGISTS	STATE HIGHWAY PATROLMEN
Assist individuals and families with mental or emotional handicaps. Conduct interviews, do counseling, refer clients to other specialists.	Study the origins, patterns of growth, behavior, organization, and characteristics of groups and institutions, including the effects of group membership on behavior. Collect, compile, analyze data; try to formulate laws of social behavior.	Enforce traffic laws; write traffic tickets; may testify in court. Investigate traffic accidents, give first aid, help motorists in trouble. Direct traffic during road repairs; check truck weights; serve as public safety information officer. Prepare reports, keep police records. May be in specialized work such as fingerprints, microscopic analysis, canine corps.
Mental health clinics, mental hospitals, child guidance centers, courts, social agencies, schools, colleges, health departments, rehabilitation centers.	Most teach and do research in colleges and universities. Others work for government agencies, research organizations, business and industrial organizations, or are self-employed as consultants.	In state police forces in 49 states (Hawaii the exception).
Undetermined.	About 10,000.	About 40,000.
A master's degree from a graduate school of social work.	Master's degree in sociology the minimum for professional positions. Ph.D. required for better positions.	Requirements vary by state. Most require high school education or equivalent. Recruits take at least 12-month training course.
Interest in and liking for people, emotional maturity, sympathy, tolerance, patience, good judgment, integrity.	Analytical ability, thoroughness, inquiring mind, emotional stability, interest in people, persistence, ability to communicate effectively.	At least 21, physical strength and courage, stamina, good health. Must pass competitive exam and meet physical and character qualifications. U.S. citizen.
College placement offices, state and local civil service commissions.	Personal recommendation of graduate professor, college placement service, civil service offices, listings in professional journals.	Apply direct to headquarters of state police. Check state civil service regulations.
Good. Can become supervisor, administrator, teacher, research worker.	Good chance to become professor, research director, administrator, consultant, lecturer-writer.	Good. Most states have merit promotion systems—pass competitive exam, advance to next rank. Typical line of advancement: private, corporal, sergeant, first sergeant, lieutenant, captain.
Start: $10,200. Experienced: to $11,300. Salaries lowest in state agencies.	Start: $10,000–$12,000. Experienced: $15,000–$25,000 or more. May add to earnings with royalties, fees.	Start: $480–$800 a month. Experienced: $640–$1100.
Demand continues to exceed supply. Excellent opportunities.	Demand increasing in all areas of employment. Best opportunities for those with Ph.D. Estimate 800 openings a year.	Rapid rise in demand anticipated. Expect 2900 openings a year throughout the 1970s.
OEK Brief No. 246 WORK Brief No. 263	OEK Brief No. 367 WORK Brief No. 301	WORK Brief No. 305

OCCUPATION	STATIONARY FIREMEN	STATISTICIANS
DUTIES	Operate and maintain steam boilers used for power or heat. Clean, oil, and grease parts. Operate mechanical devices that keep proper steam pressure in boilers; read meters; make minor repairs. May inspect equipment, light boilers, and build up steam pressure.	Collect, classify, analyze, and interpret facts stated in numerical form. Choose representative samples; plan surveys; use data as basis for decisions, predictions. May specialize in research, teaching, applied field.
WHERE EMPLOYED	In manufacturing plants; with public utilities.	Federal, local, and state government agencies; industrial establishments of all kinds; insurance companies, banks, investment companies; research organizations; colleges and universities.
NUMBER OF WORKERS	About 70,000.	About 24,000 statisticians and subprofessional assistants; more than 31% women.
EDUCATION AND TRAINING	No specific educational requirements. On-the-job training.	College degree with major in statistics, math, or economics. Graduate degree helpful for advancement.
SPECIAL QUALIFICATIONS	Normal vision, good hearing, mechanical aptitude. May have to be licensed; if so, must pass exam testing knowledge of the job.	Aptitude in math and science, reasoning ability, accuracy, ingenuity, persistence, high level of intelligence.
WAYS TO ENTER FIELD	Want ads, employment services, direct application.	Civil service offices, college placement services, employment agencies, want ads in newspapers, notices in professional journals.
CHANCE OF ADVANCEMENT	With more training or education, may advance to stationary engineer, maintenance mechanic.	Good. Can become project director, professor, administrator, consultant.
EARNINGS	Range: $2.18–$4.53 an hour. Average: $3.47.	Medians: start, $13,900; experienced 5–10 years, $14,700; experienced 30 years, $22,400.
SUPPLY AND DEMAND	Decline expected due to use of automatic, centralized equipment. Hundreds of replacement jobs will be available, however.	Field growing rapidly, good opportunities for those with proper training. Little competition for estimated 1400 openings a year.
REFERENCES	WORK Brief No. 307	OEK Brief No. 182 WORK Brief No. 308

STRUCTURAL STEEL WORKERS

Erect, position, and fasten together structural steel girders used in buildings, bridges, and other structures. Lay out work from blueprints, use rigging equipment to hoist beams, set in position, bolt or weld in place.

Most work for general contractors or structural steel contractors; others for steel companies, government agencies, public utilities, and large industrial organizations.

About 80,000 structural metal workers, almost all men.

The 3-year apprenticeship is the best way to learn the trade. High school graduation preferred but not required.

Physical strength, agility, good balance, good eyesight, spatial perception, no fear of heights.

Apply to union or contractor for apprenticeship. Watch want ads. Visit state employment office.

A few become foremen.

Journeymen average $4.65–$8.68 an hour. Apprentices start at 60% to 75% of the journeyman wage.

Demand increasing as more big buildings are built. Fairly high turnover rate, but some competition for apprenticeships. 4500 openings a year.

OEK Brief No. 304
WORK Brief No. 312

SURVEYORS

Use various instruments to measure area, distance, and elevation for mapmaking, legal, or construction purposes. Compute and record measurements, plant stakes or other markers, draw rough sketches of land areas, check work. May specialize.

Government agencies; construction, civil engineering, and architectural companies; public utilities; railroads; mining and oil companies; land surveying companies.

About 52,000; 4% women.

High school plus technical school training. College degree in surveying or civil engineering preferred.

Outdoor interests, physical stamina, ability in math, accuracy in detail work, ability to work well with others. Must pass exam for state, local licenses.

College placement services, civil service offices, state employment offices, want ads. May start as rodman, chainman, surveyor's aide. Summer job is a good way to start.

Good for those with college training. Can become chief surveyor, start own surveying or engineering company.

Start: $5500–$8100. Experienced: $8000–$11,000. Top: $12,000–$20,000.

Employment trend upward, but depends partly on construction industry, which fluctuates according to economic conditions. Expect over 2400 job openings a year.

OEK Brief No. 260
WORK Brief No. 314

SYSTEMS ANALYSTS

Plan and control work to attain maximum efficiency. Analyze organization, systems and procedures, layout, forms and reports. Make surveys, prepare flowcharts, data sheets, work plans. May specialize in electronic data processing.

Manufacturing companies, banks, insurance organizations, government agencies, department stores, other organizations. Mostly in or near industrial cities.

More than 100,000, mostly men.

College degree with courses in business, math, engineering, science. Several years business experience, especially in computer work, often required.

Intelligence, analytical ability, logical mind, initiative, business sense, human relations skills, knowledge of data processing, ability to communicate effectively.

Apply direct to employers. Want ads, civil service offices. May start in accounting, production, sales, programming.

Can become department head, executive.

Beginners: $8950–$12,700. Experienced: $14,300–$25,000 or more.

Great demand, especially for those with knowledge of data processing. Almost 28,000 openings a year—many more than qualified people to fill them.

OEK Brief No. 357
WORK Brief No. 316

OCCUPATION	TAILORS	TAXI DRIVERS
DUTIES	Make garments to order: select fabric, design; make pattern; cut and assemble parts; fit to customer; sew and finish. May specialize in one or two sewing operations, perform alterations, supervise other garment workers, design clothing.	Drive taxicab: transport passengers for fare based on time, distance, number of passengers. Pick up passengers on the street, answer radio or telephone calls. Make change, keep records. May deliver packages, luggage; act as informal guides.
WHERE EMPLOYED	Garment factories, custom tailoring shops, clothing stores, wholesale tailor shops. Some are self-employed. Cities offer the best opportunity.	Taxicab companies in towns and cities throughout U.S. Some are self-employed.
NUMBER OF WORKERS	Undetermined.	About 100,000 full time; 300,000 part time; 3% women.
EDUCATION AND TRAINING	High school plus on-the-job training or 5-year apprenticeship. Trade school may be most practical way to learn.	No minimum requirements, but high school graduates often preferred.
SPECIAL QUALIFICATIONS	Finger dexterity, good eyesight, accuracy, patience, color discrimination, sense of form, knowledge of fabrics.	Must pass exams for state, local licenses. Driving skill, good coordination and eyesight, courtesy, knowledge of driving regulations and the community. Minimum age often 21.
WAYS TO ENTER FIELD	Apply to garment factories, clothing shops. Trade school placement service, state employment agency may help. May start as hand sewer, helper.	Apply direct to cab company before getting license. Watch want ads.
CHANCE OF ADVANCEMENT	Can become custom tailor, head tailor, designer. Can open own shop.	Poor. Can become dispatcher; some switch to bus, truck driving.
EARNINGS	Vary. Depend on area, type of garment, speed, skill. Production workers in garment factories average $84.37 a week.	Most paid percentage—40%–50% of receipts. A few get a small salary plus commission. Average: $100–$125 a week plus tips.
SUPPLY AND DEMAND	Occupation is fairly stable. May be slight increase in demand for skilled workers. Apprenticeships are scarce.	Demand decreasing slightly. Many openings because of turnover. Keen competition for about 1800 jobs available each year.
REFERENCES	OEK Brief No. 24 WORK Brief No. 317	OEK Brief No. 158 WORK Brief No. 318

TEACHER AIDES

Assist classroom teachers in a variety of ways. May help arrange room, keep track of materials and supplies; sit with children during mealtimes; supervise play activities, trips; answer questions when new materials are introduced. May do clerical work, correct papers, plan group activities, work in library, run audio-visual equipment.

In elementary and secondary schools throughout the country.

More than 80,000, mostly women.

No specific educational requirements. For some jobs motherhood is the only qualification; for others some college training is necessary. Depends on what aides duties will be. On-the-job training.

Interest in children and the ability to work with them, sense of humor, patience, enthusiasm.

Direct application to school system, want ads in newspapers and teachers journals. May work part time.

Limited. Can work up to higher-paying clerical job in some school systems.

Vary considerably. Average: $2–$3 an hour. Generally low.

Outlook good, particularly in low-income areas with overcrowded classrooms.

WORK Brief No. 319

TEACHERS, ART

Give group instruction in arts and crafts, such as painting, drawing, sculpture, design. May also serve as supervisor or consultant.

In elementary and secondary public schools, private schools, museums, hospitals, and settlement houses.

Undetermined.

College degree with art major plus teaching certificate required for public school jobs. May not need degree for private school job, but must have art school training.

Artistic talent and ability, patience, enthusiasm, ability to communicate and work well with others.

Apply direct to school board or teachers agency for teaching in public schools. College placement bureau, want ads, personal recommendations also helpful.

May advance to supervisory position.

Public schools average: elementary, $9025; secondary, $9540.

Only moderate increase in jobs expected. Competition for beginning jobs—will go to applicants with best qualifications.

WORK Brief No. 23

TEACHERS, COLLEGE

Specialize in one curriculum area. Instruct students through lectures, discussions, laboratory work. Give assignments, prepare exams, grade papers. Keep informed in field, do research, write articles and books.

In the more than 2200 universities, colleges, junior colleges, professional and technical schools throughout U.S.

About 335,000; 20% women.

Graduate degree needed for most starting positions. Ph.D. essential for advancement.

Intelligence, ability to convey ideas in speech and writing, interest in subject, openness to new ideas, empathy, patience, thoroughness, responsibility, integrity.

College placement services, recommendation of graduate school professor, listings in professional journals. May start as graduate assistant.

Excellent chance to become full professor for those with doctor's degree and published research.

Average: $10,885. Range: $8000 for lecturer; $16,000 for full professor. Highest in New England and the West.

Demand much greater than number of graduates. About 10,800 additional full-time teachers will be needed each year.

OEK Brief No. 183
WORK Brief No. 69

OCCUPATION	TEACHERS, KINDERGARTEN AND ELEMENTARY SCHOOL	TEACHERS, MUSIC
DUTIES	In kindergarten, introduce science, numbers, language, social studies; use games, music, artwork. In elementary school, teach variety of subjects to one class. Plan lessons, assign work, prepare tests; grade papers; keep records; confer with parents, administrators. Most teach only one grade, but in small schools may teach several. May team-teach some subjects.	Teach students of voice, piano, or other instuments, either in groups or individually. May also serve as supervisor or consultant.
WHERE EMPLOYED	Elementary schools—public, private, and parochial—throughout U.S.	Schools, colleges, conservatories, private studios throughout U.S.
NUMBER OF WORKERS	About 1.2 million; 85% women.	About 75,000 full time.
EDUCATION AND TRAINING	College degree required in public and most other schools. 8–36 credit hours in education required, vary by states.	Special training in music. For public school teaching, bachelor's degree and teacher's certificate. In colleges, at least master's degree
SPECIAL QUALIFICATIONS	Must have state teacher's certificate. Liking for children, sympathy, energy, tact, patience, enthusiasm, emotional stability. Broad range of knowledge desirable.	Patience enthusiasm, sense of humor, ability to work well with people, love of music
WAYS TO ENTER FIELD	College placement bureaus, some state departments of education, teacher associations have information about openings. Apply to superintendent of schools.	Apply direct to school board or teacher's agency for teaching in public schools. College placement bureau, newspaper ads, personal recommendations also helpful.
CHANCE OF ADVANCEMENT	Limited. With additional training, can become counselor or principal. Can steadily increase earnings with continuous service.	Depend largely on reputation, ability to teach. Can increase earnings, become department head or administrator in school system. Open own studio.
EARNINGS	Range: $6500–$10,000 or more. Nationwide average: $9025.	In public schools and universities: $4000–$20,000. Private lessons: $1.50–$25 an hour.
SUPPLY AND DEMAND	Slight decline expected. Keen competition for beginning jobs. Best opportunities in urban ghettos, rural districts, and for teaching the handicapped.	The demand is continually increasing, especially in schools.
REFERENCES	OEK Brief No. 39 WORK Brief No. 175	OEK Brief No. 384 WORK Brief No. 169

TEACHERS, NURSERY SCHOOL

Provide supervised learning experiences for preschool children; stories, games, songs, dances, trips. May introduce social skills and attitudes, language numbers, health and safety habits. Record progress, discuss with parents.

Private, public, and church-operated nursery schools throughout U.S.

Undetermined. Almost exclusively women.

High school diploma sufficient in some states for nursery school. College degree desirable.

May need state teacher's certificate. Interest in and liking for children, knowledge of child psychology, emotional stability, patience, enthusiasm, cheerfulness.

College placement bureau can help. Apply direct to nursery school.

Limited. Can increase salary, become director of nursery school, start own school.

About $5000–$8000 a year.

Many more openings than qualified teachers. Almost no competition for those with a college degree.

OEK Brief No. 186
WORK Brief No. 219

TEACHERS, SECONDARY SCHOOL

Instruct students, plan and prepare lessons, give assignments, prepare and grade tests. Discuss problems with students, parents. Keep records. May supervise student activities. Usually specialize in one subject or several related subjects.

Public, private, and parochial junior high schools, senior high schools, and combined junior-senior high schools throughout U.S.

More than 1 million; almost half men.

Bachelor's degree in particular field of interest. Master's required in some school systems, helpful in all.

State teacher's certificate. Pleasant personality, liking for young people, understanding of their problems, fairness. Emotional stability, patience, maturity, imagination.

College placement bureau, some state education departments, and teacher associations may help. Apply to superintendent of schools or direct to principal. May start as substitute teacher.

Can increase earnings with continuous service. Can become supervisor, department head, counselor, principal.

Nationwide average: $9540. Top salaries in some states reach $15,000 or more.

Supply greater than demand. Keen competition for jobs except in physical science teaching and working with retarded or handicapped.

OEK Brief No. 5
WORK Brief No. 150

TEACHERS OF EXCEPTIONAL CHILDREN

Work with children who need special help—slow learners; the emotionally disturbed, physically handicapped, blind, deaf; those with speech problems; and the very bright. Provide group and individual experiences—may use stories, games, special equipment, audiovisual aids. Record progress, consult parents and other specialists.

In public schools, special public and private schools, hospitals, clinics, orphanages, government agencies.

Undetermined.

At least a bachelor's degree. Must take special courses to conform to state laws for teaching the handicapped.

Liking for children, warm personality, patience, understanding, flexibility, emotional maturity, sense of humor, stamina.

College placement service, teachers employment agencies, direct application to boards of education.

With graduate training and experience, can advance to director or supervisor in state or local agencies, become specialist in state departments of education.

About $200–$500 a year more than other teachers in the same school systems.

Excellent opportunities. Great shortage of trained teachers.

OEK Brief No. 138
WORK Brief No. 320

OCCUPATION	TECHNICIANS, AIR-CONDITIONING	TECHNICIANS, ATOMIC ENERGY
DUTIES	Assist engineers in research, design, development, and production of air-conditioning and refrigeration equipment. Plan and supervise installation of air-conditioning and refrigeration systems. Test and diagnose malfunctioning equipment. Supervise mechanics.	Operate nuclear reactors, particle accelerators, X-ray machines, slave manipulators, and other machines used in atomic energy industry. May monitor work areas and equipment to detect radiation, decontaminate, dispose of radioactive waste.
WHERE EMPLOYED	With manufacturers and distributors of air-conditioning and refrigeration equipment, heating, refrigeration, and air-conditioning contractors, companies and government agencies that use air-conditioning and refrigeration equipment, throughout U.S.	Atomic power plants, research labs, uranium mills, and refineries, nuclear weapons manufacturing plants, Atomic Energy Commission. Throughout U.S.; most in Tennessee, New Mexico, California, New York, Pennsylvania.
NUMBER OF WORKERS	About 650,000 engineering and science technicians; 12% women.	About 30,000 atomic energy technicians; few women.
EDUCATION AND TRAINING	High school plus 2-year program at technical institute, junior college, or university.	High school plus either some college, trade, or technical school, or on-the-job training. Physical sciences, math, electronics are important.
SPECIAL QUALIFICATIONS	Aptitude for science and math, mechanical ability, accuracy and thoroughness, persistence, problem-solving ability.	Mechanical and scientific interest and aptitude, accuracy, dependability, good health. Some must have security clearance. Civil service exam may be required.
WAYS TO ENTER FIELD	School placement bureaus, state employment agencies, newspaper want ads. Direct application to manufacturer, distributor, or contractor.	AEC in Washington has job information. State employment agencies, civil service offices list openings. Direct application may also be effective.
CHANCE OF ADVANCEMENT	Excellent. Can become specialist in design, development; go into technical sales; open own business as contractor, distributor.	Good for those with special training and education. May become foreman, chief technician; advance to higher-level technical work.
EARNINGS	Start: $5200–$8300. Experienced: $11,000 average. Sales representatives and the self-employed may make more.	Vary widely. AEC installations average: $4.11 an hour.
SUPPLY AND DEMAND	In all areas, demand for technicians is much greater than supply.	Demand increasing rapidly. Competition for the best jobs is strong. Good potential for women.
REFERENCES	OEK Brief No. 191
WORK Brief No. 8	OEK Brief No. 315
WORK Brief No. 29

TECHNICIANS, CHEMICAL

Perform routine operations in research, development, testing, analysis, and production of chemicals and related products. Help chemists and chemical engineers make computations, set up and operate apparatus, perform tests.

Most work in industries where chemistry plays an important role, such as the drug and steel industries; others for government agencies, research centers, university and hospital research laboratories.

About 650,000 engineering and science technicians; 12% women.

High school plus 1–3 years chemical technology in junior college or technical institute, or 2 years of college chemistry.

Interest in science and math, mechanical aptitude, accuracy, logical mind, patience and perseverance, tolerance for routine work, orderly work habits.

Junior college or technical school placement bureaus, want ads in newspapers, civil service offices, direct application to companies that employ technicians.

Limited. Can become supervisor, switch to technical saleswork. With more education, can become chemist or engineer.

Starting salaries: $5200–$8300. Experienced: $11,000 average.

Demand for trained technicians increasing more rapidly than supply. In many areas, several openings for every graduate. Women encouraged.

OEK Brief No. 318
WORK Brief No. 60

TECHNICIANS, DENTAL LABORATORY

Make and repair artificial teeth, crowns, bridges, braces, and other dental appliances. Work from wax impression of patient's mouth; make plaster models, castings; set teeth in denture; grind, polish. Use small hand and machine tools. May specialize.

Most work in the 7000 commercial dental laboratories that fill prescriptions for dentists. A few work directly for dentists in their offices, and the rest in government hospitals. Throughout U.S., but mostly in large cities.

About 33,500; 10% women.

High school plus 2-year program in approved technical institute or junior college plus 3 years on-the-job training, is preferred.

Mechancial aptitude, good eyesight and color discrimination, manual dexterity, patience, accuracy, attention to detail. Must pass test if certification is desired.

Usually start as trainee or apprentice. Apply directly to laboratory, dentist, or government hospital; watch want ads, check listings of employment services and dental laboratory associations.

Can specialize, become lab foreman or manager, start own commercial lab. Advancement limited in small labs.

Trainees: $78 a week. Experienced workers: $175–$225 a week. Managers and master technicians: to $300 a week.

Demand increasing somewhat for trained technicians. Average of 2900 openings a year. Competition fairly heavy for trainee positions.

OEK Brief No. 273
WORK Brief No. 88

TECHNICIANS, ELECTRONICS

Build, test, operate adjust, inspect, and repair complex electronic devices. May work with engineers in production, with scientists in research, or in repair. Usually specialize in one kind of electronic device. Keep records.

Companies that manufacture or use electronic equipment or devices, as well as government agencies, research and testing laboratories, and repair shops. Mostly in industrial regions.

Undetermined; the great majority men.

High school plus 2 years electronics in junior college or technical school, or 3–5 years formal and on-the-job training.

Interest in science and math, mechanical aptitude, problem-solving ability, accuracy, patience.

Direct application to companies is best. School placement bureaus, want ads, state employment agencies, federal Civil Service Commission also helpful.

Can become foreman, research supervisor, quality control supervisor, or (with more education) engineer or physicist.

Start: about $100 a week Experienced: to $250 a week.

Demand far exceeds supply, especially in industry. Greatest demand for those with post-high-school training. Women encouraged.

OEK Brief No. 155
WORK Brief No. 110

OCCUPATION	TECHNICIANS, PHYSICS	TECHNICIANS, RADIO-TV BROADCAST
DUTIES	Assist physicists in research, development, and testing: build and operate experimental apparatus, run routine tests, make computations, keep records, check and repair testing equipment. May specialize in one area of physics.	Set up, operate, monitor, repair, and maintain technical equipment used in radio-TV broadcasting. May specialize in maintenance, transmission, audio or video control, lighting, recording, field operations.
WHERE EMPLOYED	Industries such as aerospace, electronics, electrical equipment; government agencies, research organizations; university laboratories.	With 6500 radio and 695 TV broadcasting stations throughout U.S.
NUMBER OF WORKERS	Estimated 650,000 engineering and physical science technicians; some women.	About 20,000 men.
EDUCATION AND TRAINING	High school plus 2 or 3 years of training in college, junior college or technical school; emphasis on physics and math.	High school plus electronics courses in trade or technical school or junior college. On-the-job training often provided.
SPECIAL QUALIFICATIONS	Interest in and aptitude for science and math. Mechanical aptitude, precision, problem-solving ability, dependability	Must pass exams to get Federal Communications Commission license. Mechanical interests and aptitude, manual dexterity, mental alertness, ability to cooperate and work as member of a team.
WAYS TO ENTER FIELD	School placement bureaus, want ads in newspapers, state employment agencies, civil service offices, direct application.	Get FCC license then apply to radio or TV stations. Small stations are best starting places. Placement services of junior colleges and technical schools help in locating openings.
CHANCE OF ADVANCEMENT	Limited without additional education. Can supervise other technicians or get higher-level technical job.	Good. Move to larger station. Can become technical director, master control technician, director of engineering.
EARNINGS	Start: $5400–$8400. Experienced: $7300–$10,000. A few earn more.	Radio stations: $150–$220 a week, depending on size of station. TV stations: $140–$270 a week. Supervisors: to $13,000.
SUPPLY AND DEMAND	Demand increasing rapidly. Expect to need 5 times more than being trained. Little competition for trained men and women.	Only slight increase in openings expected because of technical advances such as automatic programming and remote control of transmitters. Competition keen for 500 openings annually.
REFERENCES	OEK Brief No. 312 WORK Brief No. 244	OEK Brief No. 302 WORK Brief No. 49

TECHNOLOGISTS, DAIRY

Test, grade, and inspect milk and milk products for quality, purity. Do research to improve old products, develop new ones. May supervise dairy production, installation and operation of dairy machinery; inspect for sanitation; teach; sell.

Dairy processing plants, manufacturers that supply dairies with machinery and accessories; public health agencies, agricultural extension services, other federal and state government agencies; colleges and universities. Throughout U.S.

About 15,000 technical workers in dairy production and related fields; 5% are women.

College degree in dairy or food technology required. Master's helpful for research or teaching.

Interest in and aptitude for science and mechanics, keen powers of observation, eye for detail, patience perseverance reliability. Must pass exam for government work.

College placement bureau, dairy industry journals, civil service offices, state employment agencies can furnish job leads. Direct application to dairy plant.

Good. Can become foreman, supervisor, research or quality-control director, inspector, administrator; switch to technical sales.

Start: about $7000. Experienced: $8500–$12,000. Top: in research and administration, $20,000 or more

Demand increasing together with increase in consumption of milk and dairy products. Little competition for beginning positions.

OEK Brief No. 214
WORK Brief No. 84

TECHNOLOGISTS, FOOD

Do research to improve quality, flavor, color, texture, nutritional value of foods. Develop new food products, improve processing and packaging techniques. Perform chemical, microbiological, taste tests; inspect for quality. May teach.

Food-processing and packing plants, manufacturers and distributors of food-processing equipment and supplies, government agencies, colleges and universities, research foundations, laboratories, trade associations.

9000 members of Institute of Food Technologists. 77% of these have technical employees under their direction.

B.S. in food technology or related science. Graduate degree becoming more important, especially for research jobs.

Scientific interests and aptitude, some mechancial and mathematical ability. Patience, accuracy, perseverance. Imagination, ingenuity helpful in research and development.

College placement service, on-campus interviews; direct application to employers; civil service offices. May start as junior technician.

Can become head of research lab, production supervisor, plant manager, administrator; switch to technical sales, teaching, consulting.

Start: $760–$1200 a month, depending on degree.

Shortage of technologists expected to continue. Almost twice as many openings as trained workers.

OEK Brief No. 215
WORK Brief No. 131

TECHNOLOGISTS, MEDICAL

Make chemical, microbiological tests of body tissues and fluids to help in the detection, diagnosis, treatment, and prevention of disease. May assist in medical or pharmaceutical research. Keep records and make reports. May specialize.

Most work in hospital laboratories; others in private laboratories, clinics, public health agencies, research institutions, industrial laboratories, and schools of medical technology.

About 44,000 registered medical technologists; 20% men.

3 years college undergraduate study plus 12 months laboratory training in medical technology school. Some colleges grant B.S.

Aptitude for and interest in science, accuracy, reliability, patience thoroughness, manual dexterity, visual perception. Must pass exam to be registered.

School placement bureaus, placement services of the two national registries, notices in medical journals are the best contacts for openings.

Limited. Can specialize, become supervisor or chief technologist, go into teaching or research.

Start: $7500 average. Government hospitals pay more than private.

Acute shortage of trained medical technologists. Graduates can usually choose from several job openings.

OEK Brief No. 32
WORK Brief No. 206

OCCUPATION	TECHNOLOGISTS, RADIOLOGIC (X-RAY)	TELEPHONE INSTALLERS
DUTIES	Take X-ray pictures of bones and internal organs for diagnosis of disease or injury. Assist radiologists in using radiation in diagnosis and treatment of disease. Operate equipment, process film, keep records. May teach.	Install telephone sets, private branch switchboards, and related equipment in homes and places of business. Climb poles, attach wires, run them into buildings, attach phones, test. Use small hand tools and testing equipment. May also locate trouble and repair customers' telephones and switchboards.
WHERE EMPLOYED	Hospitals and clinics, public health services and other government agencies, business and industrial establishments, medical and research laboratories, doctors' and dentists' offices.	With Bell System and independent telephone companies throughout U.S.
NUMBER OF WORKERS	About 80,000; about 33% men.	About 102,000 men.
EDUCATION AND TRAINING	High school plus 2 years in hospital school of X-ray technology.	High school diploma plus about 6 weeks of classroom and on-the-job training.
SPECIAL QUALIFICATIONS	Responsibility, accuracy, thoroughness, sympathy, caution, patience. Must pass exam for registration.	Mechanical aptitude, manual dexterity, pleasant appearance, good health, driving ability. May have to pass aptitude test.
WAYS TO ENTER FIELD	Hospital placement service will help. American Registry of Radiologic Technologists provides a placement service for members. Contact hospitals direct; also civil service office.	Apply direct to telephone company.
CHANCE OF ADVANCEMENT	Limited. Can become specialist, chief technologist in large hospital, instructor.	Can specialize as PBX installer or repairman. May become foreman or supervisor.
EARNINGS	Start: $110–$190 a week.	Average: $3.62 an hour for installers; $3.96 for repairmen.
SUPPLY AND DEMAND	More jobs available than trained technicians. Almost no competition for beginning positions.	Employment in this occupation should continue to increase. PBX installers and repairmen in special demand. About 5300 openings a year expected.
REFERENCES	OEK Brief No. 37 WORK Brief No. 340	OEK Brief No. 359 WORK Brief No. 322

TELEPHONE OPERATORS	THERAPISTS, INHALATION	THERAPISTS, OCCUPATIONAL
Assist customers and other operators in placing calls. Long-distance operators place calls by means of switchboard or key set; keep records; may compute charges. Information operators look up telephone numbers for customers.	Administer oxygen, carbon dioxide, and aerosol medication to patients, carrying out physicians' instructions. May explain techniques and apparatus to nurses and interns, or teach in formal training program.	Guide educational, vocational, and recreational activities of patients with mental or physical handicaps to stimulate their interest and feelings of accomplishment, aid them in their recovery, and perhaps prepare them for future occupations.
With Bell System and independent telephone companies throughout U.S.	Almost all work in hospitals.	Hospitals, clinics, curative workshops, rehabilitation centers, homes for the aged, nursing homes, schools and camps for handicapped children, homes of patients who cannot come to a center, and the armed forces.
About 252,000; mostly women.	About 10,000—mostly men—are employed in this work. About 4000 are registered therapists and certified technicians.	About 7500 occupational therapists. Most are women.
High school diploma preferred. Several weeks of on-the-job training provided by employer.	High school graduation plus 2-year program in hospital school of inhalation therapy and 1-year internship. Must pass exam given by professional association to become registered or certified.	Bachelor's degree plus 9 or 10 months clinical training. If degree not in occupational therapy, additional 18 months training.
Good eyesight and hearing, manual dexterity, mental alertness, pleasant voice, courtesy, patience, tact.	Physical and emotional stamina, ability to meet emergencies calmly, strong sense of responsibility, mechanical aptitude, liking for people.	Emotional stability, patience, liking for and interest in people, physical stamina, cheerful nature, imagination, enthusiasm. Must pass exam for registration.
Apply direct to personnel office of telephone company, or to chief operator of branch office or exchange. Start part time before graduation.	The training school usually places its graduates. Check ads in Inhalation Therapy journal; apply direct to hospitals.	Placement bureaus of colleges and universities. American Occupational Therapy Assn., state employment agencies. Apply to hospitals, clinics.
Fair. Can become service assistant, chief operator; switch to clerical job with the telephone company.	May become teacher in hospital school. Some advance to head of a hospital's inhalation therapy department.	Can specialize, teach; become senior therapist, director of therapy department, consultant
U.S. average for trainee, $2.16 an hour; experienced, $2.25; chief operator, $4.24.	Start: about $555 a month. Top: $830 a month.	Average annual salary for staff therapist: $8000–$10,000. Top for administrator: about $18,000.
Employment declining because of increasing automation of service but always many openings for replacements.	Urgent demand for therapists, since there are comparatively few trained people. Expect 2100 job openings a year throughout the 1970s.	Need about 1150 occupational therapists a year. Demand continues to be far greater than supply of trained newcomers as health facilities improve. More and more men are entering the occupation.
OEK Brief No. 20 WORK Brief No. 323	OEK Brief No. 388 WORK Brief No. 166	OEK Brief No. 73 WORK Brief No. 221

OCCUPATION	THERAPISTS, PHYSICAL	THERAPISTS, SPEECH AND HEARING
DUTIES	Work to rehabilitate persons with muscle, nerve, joint, or bone disease or injury Use massage, heat treatments, radiation, electrical and mechanical devices according to doctor's prescription. Teach use of artificial limbs, braces, crutches. Help patient exercise	Through tests, interview, and observation, determine patient's speech or hearing disorder or problem, its cause, and appropriate treatment. Perform or supervise corrective work with children and adults; may teach, do research.
WHERE EMPLOYED	Most work in hospitals; others in public health agencies, rehabilitation centers, doctors' offices, schools for the handicapped, clinics, schools of physical therapy.	Elementary and secondary schools, hospitals, medical centers, university and private clinics, special community agencies that deal with mental health, guidance, psychological problems, and related subjects.
NUMBER OF WORKERS	About 15,000; 20% men.	About 22,000 qualified therapists. Many more women than men.
EDUCATION AND TRAINING	College degree in physical therapy, or degree in another subject plus 12 to 18 months in certificate program.	College degree with major in speech pathology. Certification for clinical competency by American Speech and Hearing Assn. requires master's degree or equivalent study.
SPECIAL QUALIFICATIONS	Outgoing personality, emotional stability, tact, sympathy, patience, cheerful disposition, desire to help people manual dexterity. License required in most states.	Sincere interest in people and desire to help them overcome problems. Patience, perseverance, imagination, sense of humor, good speech habits, well-modulated voice, warm and friendly personality that inspires confidence.
WAYS TO ENTER FIELD	College placement service, want ads helpful. Apply direct to hospitals, clinics, civil service offices.	Get leads from university placement service. Apply direct to school districts, hospitals, medical centers, private and university speech and hearing clinics.
CHANCE OF ADVANCEMENT	Chances good to become chief therapist, supervisor; switch to teaching or research work.	Become an administrator, concentrate on research, combine paid employment with private practice, shift to private practice exclusively.
EARNINGS	Beginners: average $8500. Experienced: $14,000–$20,000. Administrators: $15,000–$25,000.	Beginners with B.S. degree, no experience: $6400. With master's or several years of experience: $9900 or more. Top: $15,000 and up.
SUPPLY AND DEMAND	Critical shortage of therapists. Rapidly growing field with high turnover. Competition negligible. Men encouraged. About 1600 openings a year expected.	There is a need for thousands more of these specialized workers. Demand is much greater than the number of graduates.
REFERENCES	OEK Brief No. 76 WORK Brief No. 241	OEK Brief No. 148 WORK Brief No. 304

TOOL AND DIE MAKERS	TRAVEL AGENTS	TRUCK DRIVERS, LOCAL
Construct, repair, and test machine tools, jigs, fixtures, gauges, dies, molds, and other metal implements. Lay out work, cut and shape stock, finish, assemble, test. Use hand and machine tools, precision measuring devices.	Help travelers plan itineraries; arrange for transportation, sightseeing, lodging, meals. Give information, advice; make reservations and get tickets; figure costs and arrange financing; plan, arrange, and sell tours. Itinerary workers usually specialize on trips in certain countries or areas.	Load truck, drive to destination, unload, get signed receipt. May have helpers to load and unload truck. Keep records of trips, deliveries, maintenance, and repairs. May collect money, make change.
Machinery manufacturing industries, other industrial plants, tool and die job or production shops. Mostly in industrial areas: California, Ohio, Michigan, New York, Pennsylvania, Illinois.	Commercial travel agencies, automobile clubs, state and local travel bureaus (often part of the chamber of commerce); travel bureau of airlines, railroads, bus companies, shipping companies. Mostly in cities.	Wholesale and retail businesses; industrial companies, construction companies, freight and express agencies, government agencies, and trucking companies. Some are self-employed.
About 165,000; less than 1% women.	Estimated 10,000–12,000 agents, men and women.	About 1.2 million, mostly men.
High school plus 4- or 5-year apprenticeship or longer period of on-the-job training. Trade or technical school training helpful.	High school diploma essential, some college preferred. Large agencies may give about 6 months of on-the-job training.	No definite education requirements. May be given a week or more of on-the-job training.
Mechanical ability, manual dexterity, accuracy, thoroughness, mathematical ability, spatial perception, ability to read blueprints and follow instructions exactly, patience.	Sales ability, pleasing personality, neat appearance, travel experience, liking for people, attention to detail, patience, courtesy.	Must get state, local licenses. Excellent driving ability, good eyesight and coordination, physical strength and stamina. Alertness, caution, reliability, courtesy are desirable.
Watch want ads. Apply to union office, state employment service or direct to shops and factories. Trade school placement office may be helpful.	Apply direct to automobile club, airline, travel bureau, or agency. May start in clerical job—as ticket agent, secretary—or as tour guide.	Apply direct to companies that hire truck drivers. Watch want ads. State employment agency may help. May start as substitute driver, helper.
Can become tool designer, foreman, supervisor, plant manager, machine-tool salesman; open own tool and die shop.	Can become manager; open own agency. Mostly by moving to a better job with another agency.	Limited. Can increase earnings by driving heavier or long-distance truck; become dispatcher, routeman, manager; start own trucking company.
Journeymen: $3 45–$5.29 an hour. Apprentices start at 50%–65% of journeyman wage.	Range: $300–$700 or more a month. Some agents are paid salary plus commission.	$3.63–$5.17 an hour, depending on city, size and type of truck, products hauled.
Excellent opportunities. Fairly rapid increase in demand as more machine tools are used in automated production lines. About 4700 openings a year.	Increased travel means greater demand for agents. Competition keen for entry, advancement.	Moderate increase in employment foreseen. About 15,000 openings a year, mostly because of turnover.
OEK BRIEF No. 198 WORK Brief No. 325	OEK Brief No. 100 WORK Brief No. 328	

OCCUPATION	TRUCK DRIVERS, LONG-DISTANCE	TYPISTS AND STENOGRAPHERS
DUTIES	Inspect truck before and after trip, drive tractor-trailer between towns and cities, make minor repairs, keep records and make reports. May supervise loading and unloading.	Type letters, envelopes, reports, lists, stencils, and the like. May take dictation in shorthand and transcribe or use dictating machine for transcription. May have general clerical duties such as filing, answering telephone, keeping records, operating business machines.
WHERE EMPLOYED	Private carriers—companies that transport their own goods and products—and for-hire trucking companies (either common or contract carriers). Some men own their trucks.	Business, industry, government agencies, and sizable nonprofit organizations throughout U.S.
NUMBER OF WORKERS	About 655,000 men.	About 700,000 typists; 2.8 million in jobs requiring stenographic skills; less than 5% men.
EDUCATION AND TRAINING	Grade school education plus 2 years high school often required. Driver-training course or trade school helpful.	High school diploma usually required. Business school training helpful. Type 40–50 words a minute.
SPECIAL QUALIFICATIONS	State chauffeur's license needed. Good eyesight, hearing, health; at least 21 years old, 1–5 years driving experience (preferably on trucks or buses). May have to pass road test. Must be able to read and speak English.	Finger dexterity, hand-eye coordination, accuracy, clerical ability, dependability, ability to follow instructions, knowledge of spelling and punctuation.
WAYS TO ENTER FIELD	Get experience as a local truck or bus driver. Then apply to trucking companies, private carriers. Watch want ads, visit state employment office.	School placement service, employment agencies, want ads. Apply direct to organizations. Try federal, state, local civil service offices.
CHANCE OF ADVANCEMENT	Limited. Mostly by getting preferred runs. Can become dispatcher, driver trainer, supervisor, safety director.	Can learn to operate another kind of office machine requiring more skill; become secretary, correspondent, supervisor, office manager.
EARNINGS	Usually paid on mileage-hourly basis. Average: $12,600 a year.	Typists: average $457 a month. Stenographers: average $461–$526.
SUPPLY AND DEMAND	Moderate increase in employment expected, though there will be considerable competition for 21,000 expected openings.	Demand constantly exceeds supply, especially for those who can operate special office machines. Expect 100,000 openings annually. Turnover rate high.
REFERENCES	OEK Brief No. 57 WORK Brief No. 191	OEK Brief No. 252 WORK Brief No. 330

UPHOLSTERERS

Cover furniture, vehicle seats, mattresses, caskets with any of a variety of materials. May cut material, sew it together, place springs in frame, cover springs with burlap, install filling or padding, attach covering and trimming. In factory, workers specialize; in custom shop, one person may do all steps.

Furniture, bedding, casket manufacturers; auto, aircraft, railroad, and bus builders. Most located in industrial centers throughout U.S. In custom upholstering and repair shops in cities of all sizes.

About 33,000 furniture upholsterers; 9000 automobile upholsterers. Women employed especially for cutting and sewing.

High school graduation preferred, not required. Vocational and trade schools offer upholstering programs. Most shops train on the job for few months to year or more. Limited number of 3-year apprenticeships.

Good eyesight, manual dexterity, neatness and orderly work habits, good sense of color, artistic ability, spatial perception.

Apply direct to furniture or other manufacturers employing upholsterers. Watch newspaper want ads, check with state and private employment agencies and with local upholsterers union. Inquire at local custom furniture and repair shops for helper job.

Advancement opportunities rather limited; may become foreman or supervisor, plant manager. Operating one's own shop may be advantageous but involves considerable economic risk; many fail each year.

In furniture: start, $1.60–$2.50; experienced, $3–$5.25. In auto industry: start $1.60–$2.25; experienced, $2.30–$6.25.

Shortage of qualified workers in many areas. Expect high level of production to continue so job prospects appear good.

OEK Brief No. 130
WORK Brief No. 331

VETERINARIANS

Prevent, diagnose, treat, and control animal diseases. Protect public from diseases carried by animals or animal products. Give advice on animal breeding and care. May specialize in livestock, pets; teach; do research.

More than ⅔ are in private practice. Others employed by agricultural colleges, schools of veterinary medicine, government agencies, pet hospitals, drug and animal-food manufacturers, zoos, ranches, and the like.

About 25,000; 2% women.

At least 2 years college plus 4 years in school of veterinary medicine.

Liking for and interest in animals, scientific aptitude , excellent powers of observation, physical stamina, friendliness, tact. Must pass exam for state license.

Apply to established veterinarians; civil service offices. Placement bureau of veterinary college may be helpful. Can start own practice.

Can start and expand own practice; become professor, research director, administrator, consultant.

Government: start, $10,539–$11,905; experienced, $13,500–$26,700. Salaries higher in private practice.

Supply of graduates does not meet the demand for about 1500 a year. Some competition to enter veterinary school, however. Women encouraged.

OEK Brief No. 139
WORK Brief No. 334

VOCATIONAL REHABILITATION COUNSELORS

Help physically and mentally handicapped persons to become employable. May arrange for medical diagnosis; medical, surgical, or psychiatric treatment; provision, fitting, and training in use of artificial limbs and other corrective devices. Counsel regarding employment, arrange for special vocational training, place in suitable job, follow up on progress.

Federal agencies, especially Veterans Administration and Office of Vocational Rehabilitation; state rehabilitation agencies; homes and schools for handicapped; organizations such as National Foundation—March of Dimes.

About 13,000; 20% women.

Bachelor's degree in vocational guidance; graduate work desirable. Some jobs require Ph.D. VA and Vocational Rehabilitation Administration provide financial assistance for graduate study.

Strong interest in people and their problems, cheerful disposition, optimistic outlook, sympathy, tolerance, patience, convincing and inspiring personality.

Apply to personnel officer of government agencies and to private organizations.

Start as junior counselor, become counselor, supervisor, administrator; specialize in one area of service, such as vocational training.

Median in state agencies: $7800–$10,000 a year. Average with Ph.D.: $18,900.

Demand far exceeds the supply. About half the number needed to fill current openings are being graduated each year.

WORK Brief No. 335

OCCUPATION	WAITERS AND WAITRESSES	WELDERS
DUTIES	Serve food and beverages; answer questions about the menu, offer suggestions, take orders, serve meals, figure and present checks. May set and clear tables, fill containers, prepare beverages and short orders, take payment and make change.	Join two or more pieces of metal by applying intense heat (and often pressure), using hand-welding equipment or welding machines. Cut, trim, shape metal. May specialize as electric-arc, gas, or resistance welders, or oxygen cutters.
WHERE EMPLOYED	Eating establishments of all kinds such as restaurants, cafeterias, hotel and motel dining rooms, private clubs, bars, cocktail lounges, diners, tearooms, and sandwich shops.	Factories that manufacture metal products, metalworking shops, government agencies (such as road and public works commissions), construction companies, railroads, public utilities. Mostly in industrial areas.
NUMBER OF WORKERS	About 1 million; 90% waitresses.	About 535,000 welders and cutters; a few women.
EDUCATION AND TRAINING	No definite educational requirements. A few weeks of on-the-job training sometimes given. May start as a busboy or busgirl.	High school preferred. Trade school plus 2 or more years of on-the-job training required to become skilled welder.
SPECIAL QUALIFICATIONS	May need health certificate. Neat appearance, pleasant personality, good memory, alertness, tact, ability to work under pressure, physical stamina.	Manual dexterity, mechanical ability, good eyesight, thoroughness, physical stamina, coordination. May have to pass exam for certification, license.
WAYS TO ENTER FIELD	Apply direct to restaurants, other eating establishments. Watch want ads. Visit state employment agency.	Placement office of trade school, union offices, state employment service, newspaper want ads give information about openings. Direct application. May start as helper.
CHANCE OF ADVANCEMENT	Transfer to larger establishment. Some chance to become headwaiter, cashier, host or hostess.	Good. Can become skilled combination welder, inspector, foreman, technician; start own repair shop.
EARNINGS	Usually wages plus tips, free meals. Wage range: $.82–$2.15 an hour. In busy restaurants, tips total more than wages.	$2.81–$3.74 an hour.
SUPPLY AND DEMAND	At least 67,000 openings a year. Number of waitresses increasing, waiters declining. Turnover high among women. Keen competition for jobs in places where tips are good.	Skilled welders in great demand. Training and education will be increasingly important to fill 22,000 job openings a year.
REFERENCES	OEK Brief No. 267 WORK Brief No. 336	OEK Brief No. 199 WORK Brief No. 338

WILDLIFE MANAGERS

Develop and maintain natural food and shelter for wildlife, usually in refuge or conservation area. Determine wildlife inhabitants, take census, improve refuge as needed; restock streams, encourage breeding, remove surplus animals through regulated hunting, trap animals to restock other areas; keep records, make reports, supervise employees.

2/3 of all wildlife workers are employed by state agencies; 15%–20% by U.S., mostly in Fish and Wildlife Service; others in conservation societies, hunting-fishing clubs, commercial fisheries, and fur farms.

Number undetermined. Some women in research, biological experimentation, banding, hatchery, office work.

Bachelor's degree with major in biology, zoology, fishery science, or wildlife management. Summer work on farm, forestry camp, biological station offers good training.

Love of outdoor life and animals is essential. Good health, physical stamina important. For federal government employment, must be U.S. citizen.

Check with federal and state civil service offices for information on required written competitive exam. Contact Wildlife Management Institute, Wildlife Society. Look for job opportunities in *Journal of Wildlife Management*. Apply direct to private and commercial organizations.

Promotion in government work not rapid, because this is highly specialized career service. May become administrator, teach, do research.

Federal starting salaries, $7300–$14,000, depending on degree.

Steady increase in employment opportunities, and demand for trained personnel expected to continue as government wildlife and conservation programs expand.

OEK Brief No. 149
WORK Brief No. 339

WRITERS, FREE-LANCE

Write stories, articles, reports, verse for sale to publishers as books, texts, pamphlets or for use in books, magazines, newspapers. May do research, travel, interview people. May use typewriter, tape recorder, camera and other photographic equipment.

Self-employed. May get assignments or requests for specific piece of writing from publishers.

Undetermined.

Most writers have had some college training and have read extensively. Many attend workshops, classes, writers conferences from time to time.

Talent for getting people to talk and for reporting accurately; broad knowledge. Self-discipline, perseverance, patience. Qualifications for salaried job by which to earn a living until self-employment is economically feasible.

Many free-lance hopefuls work first as college English teachers or in publishing, advertising, journalism, public relations, films, or television. Participate in writers contests. Write, write, write, and keep submitting material to appropriate publishers.

Each new letter of acceptance is advancement. Bigger checks from better magazines. Be published enough, in right places, to become authority on a subject or become a "name" author.

Median yearly incomes are very low. Only small number earn $5000 or more annually.

Not hard for truly good writers to find acceptance of their material, but even the talented find competition extremely keen.

OEK Brief No. 275
WORK Brief No. 136

WRITERS, TECHNICAL

Present scientific, technical information in clear, logical, factual writing. Do research; write articles, reports, manuals, pamphlets, instructions, and the like. May edit, rewrite technical writings of scientists, engineers.

Trade magazines, professional and technical journals, manufacturing companies, government agencies, universities, research foundations, companies that specialize in technical writing, large city newspapers, wire services.

About 20,000 technical writers and editors.

College degree with courses in science, engineering, journalism, and liberal arts. On-the-job training.

Writing ability, interest in science and technology, logical mind, thoroughness, analytical ability, human-relations skills.

College placement bureau, civil service offices, employment agencies. Watch want ads in newspapers, professional and technical journals.

Can become supervisor, editor. With experience, can become consultant; write free-lance articles on technical subjects.

Start: $6000–$8000 a year. Experienced: $8000–$16,000. Top: about $20,000.

Demand growing for writers with scientific or engineering backgrounds, especially in electronics and communications. Some competition for liberal arts graduates.

OEK Brief No. 286
WORK Brief No. 321

INDEX